Dedicated to my husband; my light, my fire, my midnight sun.

Around the Ring Road:

A Photographic Travel Guide
to Navigating Iceland in Eight Days

WHEN MY HUSBAND first asked me where I wanted to go on our honeymoon, I did not even have to think twice. Without knowing more than a handful of tidbits about Iceland, I felt drawn to the little island whose volcanoes once outnumbered its first inhabitants. Sensing a tinge of reluctance on his behalf, I urged him to leave the matter of planning in my hands, and within days the photos we discovered solidified the decision. This is where the conundrum began. There appeared to be an abundance of photography at my disposal, but information was scarce and scattered. Once I discovered the existence of a road that encompassed the entire circumference of Iceland, I knew that this would be our gateway to see a little bit of everything in a short amount of time.

Route 1, better known as the Ring Road, a stretch 1,332 km in length, connects most of Iceland's major sight, making them as accessible and convenient as a drive-thru. Further research unveiled a popular route totaling 300km known as the Golden Circle, and thus our itinerary began to take shape.

After seven months of research, we set out armed with several pages of hand-drawn maps, countless scribbled notes, and, what my husband suspected, was too much camera equipment. The first day into our journey we had a hunch that we would want to come back. By the last day I said "Auf Wiedersehen," knowing we would one day see Iceland once again.

I have compiled this book, because I wanted to share the innumerable hours of research I placed into planning our trip, so that others could have these resources at their fingertips. I was hesitant at first of whether or not I was capable of undertaking such a large endeavor. Each day, I worked on this book with the same tenacity and delight I experienced during my travels in Iceland.

I wish you sunshine and safe traveling on your own Icelandic adventures.

All the best,
Aleksandra Stone

CONTENT

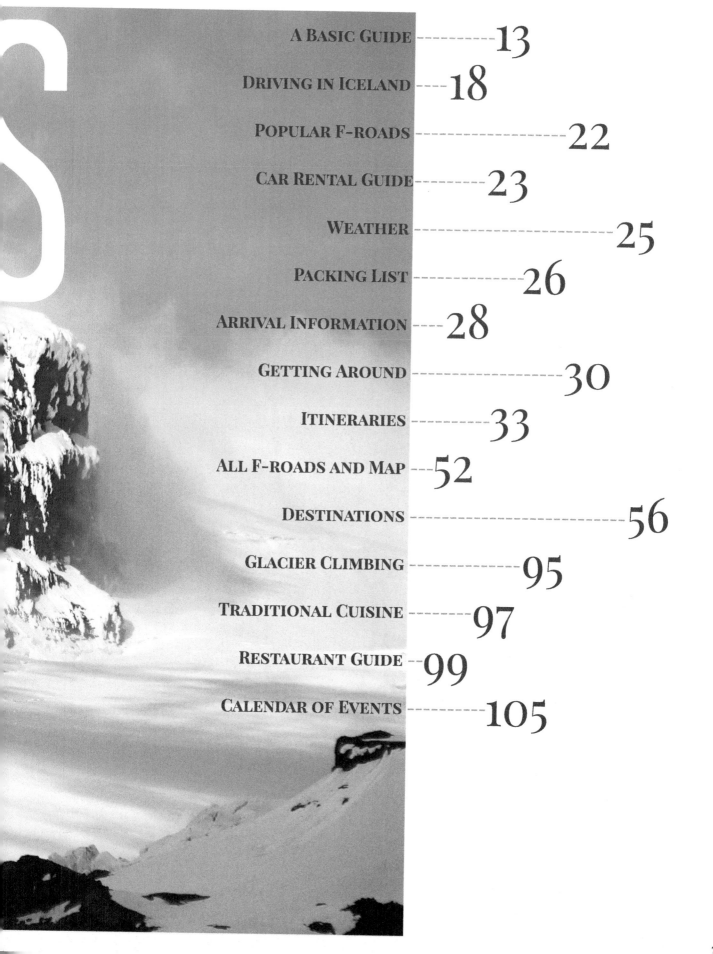

A Basic Guide ----------- 13

Driving in Iceland ---- 18

Popular F-roads ------------ 22

Car Rental Guide ---------- 23

Weather ------------ 25

Packing List ----------- 26

Arrival Information ----- 28

Getting Around ------------ 30

Itineraries -------- 33

All F-roads and Map --- 52

Destinations ---------------- 56

Glacier Climbing ------- 95

Traditional Cuisine -------- 97

Restaurant Guide --- 99

Calendar of Events ---------- 105

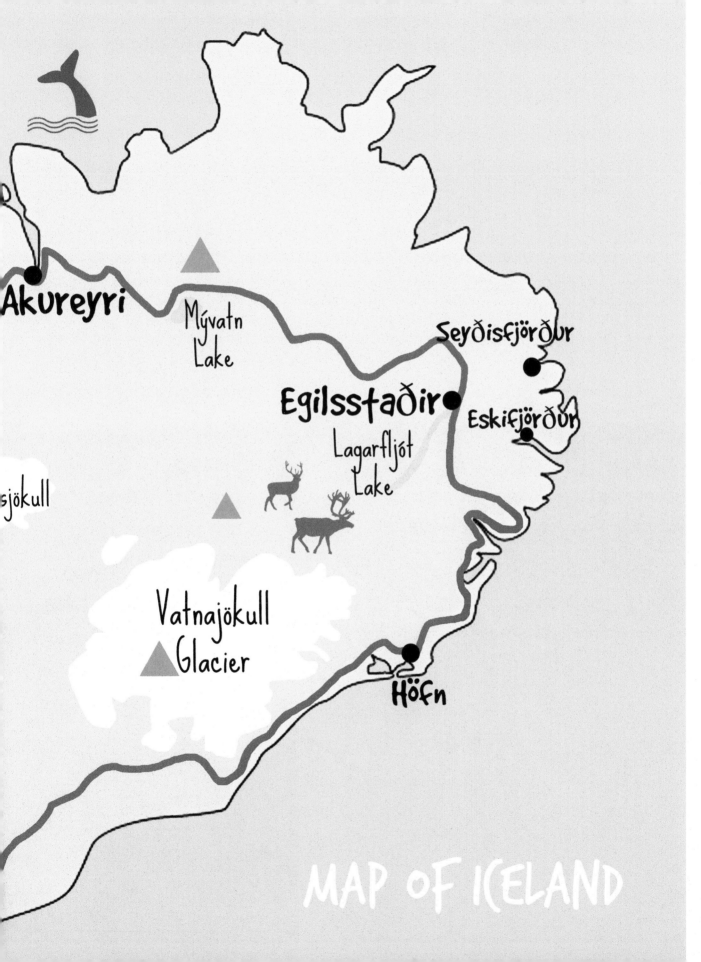

MAP OF ICELAND

HIGH SEASON
June-August
SHOULDER SEASON
April, May, September, October
OFF SEASON
November- March

Visit

Iceland

WHEN TO

ICELAND HAS A DEFINITIVE TOURIST SEASON beginning in June and concluding in August. These three summer months coincide with the average opening dates for Iceland's many F-roads, which are in large part inaccessible much of the year without heavily modified cars. Iceland, however, is a land of great natural beauty no matter the season, with tourists coming even in the dead of winter to observe the brilliant illuminations of the Aurora Borealis.

If you are traveling to take full advantage of the rugged mountain terrains with a 4x4 vehicle and wish to leave with no sight unseen, the best time to for you to travel is during the high season.

However, if your intentions are to navigate the Ring Road with a 2x2 vehicle, deviating very little from the circumference of the Route 1, the shoulder season will provide you with some of the best deals in airfare and car rental prices. Many of the major sights, such as the ones in the Golden Circle, will still be accessible via a standard car, with a fraction of the cost for accommodations.

If you wish to see the Northern Lights, the best months are September through mid-April. While November-February may seem like a sure bet because they offer the darkest night sky, the weather is often unrelenting and harsh. Aurora forecasts are available at www.northernlightsiceland.com.

ICE LAND

A BASIC GUIDE TO THE LAND OF *Fire and Ice*

Language: Icelandic (íslenska)

English is compulsory in Icelandic schools, and is therefore widely understood in Iceland. You should have no trouble communicating with people working in the customer service industry as they have become used to tourist encounters. While most people in well-populated areas have a proficient grasp of the English language, you may encounter difficulties communicating with locals from small and remote farms.

Currency: Icelandic króna (Ikr)
Coins come in denominations of 1, 5, 10, 50 and 100.
Banknotes are issued as 500, 1000, 2000, 5000 and 10,000 .

Money: Plastic is the way to go for anything in Iceland, but if you truly feel more at ease by carrying a bit of cash, I recommend exchanging no more than 10,000 ISK (about 87.00 USD) at the Keflavik International Airport. This should cover any unexpected scenarios dealing with malfunctioning POS terminals.

Iceland: (Ísland)

This strikingly beautiful Nordic country of 320,000 inhabitants enjoys a mild climate, and seemingly omnipresent and profuse vegetation, in the presence of countless fjords, rugged lava fields, glaciers, and volcanoes.

Time: Iceland is on Greenwich Mean Time (GMT), and does not adjust to daylight savings time.

In 1918 Iceland declared its independence from Danish rule.

Banks:

Currency exchange is available at all banks around the country. Banks in Iceland are generally open 9 am – 4 pm, Monday through Friday, with the exception of public holidays.

Prices: Because of the 2008 economic crisis, Iceland has become slightly more affordable. Nevertheless, many consumer goods must be imported and are therefore subject to a high VAT and exorbitant import duties. In addition, petrol prices are amongst the most expensive in the world.

Credit and Debit: The use of credit cards is more common here than in many European countries. Twenty-four hour ATMs are available in even the most remote towns. Settling your debts electronically is the best way to go, so there is little to no need to make a large currency exchange at Keflavik International Airport. Self-service petrol stations, solar powered road side vending machines, and even remote guest houses, accept Visa, MasterCard, Maestro, Cirrus, and AMEX cards. You will only need a PIN code or an EMV chipped card to obtain goods at unmanned petrol stations. To obtain a PIN code for a standard issue US credit card without an EMV chip, simply call your card issuer and request to add a magstripe PIN for that particular card.

Pre-paid Gas Cards

Pre-paid gas cards are available during daytime operating hours at all N1, Shell, and Orkan service stations. It is advisable to keep your car adequately fueled because there are many wide gaps between fuel service stations along the Ring Road. The N1 is the most numerous petrol station in Iceland. Like many others, it remains open 24 hours a day, but is unmanned from 10:00pm to 8:00 am. Pre-paid denominations for most cards are 1,000, 5000, and 10,000. When you swipe your card at the self service station you will be asked the maximum amount of money you wish to spend from your pre-paid card, however you will only be charged for the amount that is actually pumped. I advise that you keep a N1 card with at least the minimal balance at all times while driving the Ring Road.

Pre-paid SIM Cards

Access to a telephone is never a bad thing, especially if you are far away or in distress. Rental cars may be prone to just about anything on the rough terrain. Consider getting the smallest bundle, in case you need assistance.

There are two major phone companies in Iceland, Siminn and Vodafone, both of which offer prepaid SIM cards that are suitable for a short stay in Iceland.

You may purchase a pay-as-you-go SIM card from a Síminn store at Keflavík Airport or at Tourist Information. They are also sold at 10/11 convenience stores and gas stations. You may buy a Vodafone card at the duty free shop in the arrival hall in Keflavík Airport, Vodafone stores in town, or at a gas station. For more info visit: www.vodafone.is/en/prepaid/ or www.siminn.is/english/

Groceries

Stock up on food at the budget grocery store before heading out on the Ring Road. Iceland's budget grocery chains, Bónus or Krónan are typically open from 10 am to 6 pm, with varying weekend and holiday hours.

In rural areas, the most common grocery chain is Samkaup and Netto. Most major gas stations around the country such as N1 also include convenience stores with basic food items and small cafeterias serving hamburgers, fries, hot dogs, and pizza. If you are planning bringing your own lunch to each sight, keep in mind the closing times of local grocery stores. Because of the odd hours of operation, in most cases you have to purchase your lunch items the day before.

Laundry

In downtown Reykjavík, self-service laundry facilities can be found at the Laundromat Cafe on Austurstræti 9 (for dining guests) or at KEX Hostel on Skúlugata 28 (open to the public).

Pharmacies:

are called apótek or lyfjaverslun in Icelandic and are located in most towns around the island. Hours of operation are normally 10am – 6pm, Monday through Friday. Saturday 10am– 4pm.

Electrical Outlets

Electricity in Iceland is standard European: 240 Volts, alternating at 50 cycles per second . Iceland uses the Europlug/Schuko-Plug, which consists of two round prongs.

Most laptops will automatically work with 220 volts (check the back of your laptop for power input markings). That means, you'll only need an adapter to change the shape of your power plug to fit into an outlet in Iceland.

Tip: Heat producing devices, hair dryers in particular, run on varying voltages. It is best to skip bring one altogether and check if your accommodation can provide one for your use.

Public Holidays

You will find that most shops, banks, and businesses are closed or have reduced hours on the following holidays: Christmas Eve, Christmas, New Year's Eve, New Year's Day, Maundy Thursday, Good Friday, Easter Sunday, Easter Monday, First Day of Summer (Late April), Labor Day (May 1st), Ascension Day, Whit Sunday, Whit Monday, National Day (June 17th), Bank Holiday (First Monday in August).

Weather

For public weather alerts and day-to-day forecasts visit http://en.vedur.is/

US Embassy

Laufásvegur 21, Reykjavik, Iceland

Tourist Information

If you are in need of additional assistance and information, visit the official tourist information center in Reykjavik.

Tourist Information Centre
Adalstraeti 2
Reykjavik, Iceland
www.visitreykjavik.is

Iceland's Tourism Website:

www.visiticeland.com/

British Embassy

Laufásvegur 31
Reykjavik, Iceland

Smoking Ordinances:

Smoking in public establishments, such as restaurants, bars, night clubs, and public transportation is strictly prohibited. These establishments do not provide designated outdoor smoking areas. If you plan on smoking outside, keep a reasonable distance from the entryway.

Car Rental

Public transportation is scarce outside of Reykjavik and Akureyri . Touring the Ring Road by car is the easiest and most viable option for tourists to make their way around the island. It will however take up a significant amount of your budget. Tour bus companies will only take you to certain destinations, and the cost of hopping from tour to tour adds up quickly. With an abundance of car rental companies in Iceland, you are guaranteed to find a good deal that will not blow your budget.

Go Online

The best deals car rental deals may be found online. Do not wait to get to Iceland to look for a car. Know your options and comparison shop. Some companies even offer discounts if you book online.

Note

When renting a car, consider the following two options, as they will in part influence the entire outcome of your trip. The decision to rent either a 2x2 or a 4x4 will affect your budget and your sight seeing abilities significantly.

2X2

Consider renting a 2x2 if you are absolutely certain that you will be able to resist the tempting side roads marked with point of interest indicators. These roads are never paved and you will not have the freedom to explore them without inflicting some type of damage to the undercarriage of a low-lying 2x2. If your goal is to travel strictly around the perimeter of the Golden Circle, Diamond Circle and the Ring Road you will encounter no difficulties with a simple 2x2 car, and your budget will be thankful for it.

4X4

The lure of the F-road is akin to a Siren's call. If you rent a 4x4 vehicle, you will have the freedom to take such a road. If you are traveling during the high or shoulder season, a small 4x4 is great for moderate exploration of the open F-roads. If you are traveling during the off season, or want indulge in some heavy exploration of the F-roads you will have to consider getting a modified 4x4. A snorkel is not necessary during the high season, as most streams are navigable in a non-modified 4x4. If there is one expense that I personally think should not be spared, it is the additional cost of renting a 4x4.

Insurance

Most companies do not insure the undercarriage of the car, so make smart decisions, even with a 4x4. Inspect the undercarriage of the car you are receiving; you do not want to be held liable for someone else's damage. Theft insurance is unnecessary as Iceland is an incredibly safe country with very little car theft. Sand and ash insurance is discretionary, and most companies offer it. I suggest purchasing it if you have the budget to spare, and require the piece of mind. If you intend on exploring F-roads with your 4x4, it is wise to consider the windshield protection. As with all things, driving with care and keeping a good distance from other cars will limit chances of windshield damage.

Note

The longer you keep your car the cheaper it becomes by the day.

Driving in Iceland

If you are driving on the Ring Road and/or the Golden/Diamond circle, the trip is fairly straightforward. Almost all of the Ring Road is paved, with the exception of very small sections of smooth gravel roads, which 2x2's are able to maneuver on.
The speed limit and road signs are labeled very clearly, and stand out against the landscape.

Highland driving, however, may be a bit tricky as road conditions depend on the season and the weather. Even in the summer, road conditions may change quickly, and you may find yourself unable to cross a stream after a downpour of rain. If you are planning on traveling on an F-road, always make certain the road is first open before planning your day out.

Off-Road Driving:

UNLESS YOU ARE DRIVING ON A MARKED F–ROAD,
it is illegal to drive off-road. Due to a very short growing season,
off-roading leads to irreparable damage to the fragile Icelandic
environment, and can take decades to correct and recover. Taking
an unmarked road with a visible trail made by other cars is punishable
by very high fines. Such roads lead to soil erosion, water diversion, and
vegetation damage. With only a limited amount of sunlight, it takes
years for damaged moss beds to re-grow.

Fuel

In Iceland, petrol is sold by the liter not the gallon; therefore, expect to pay about $9 per gallon.

Crossing a River

Once the snow begins to thaw, brooks and streams turn in to swiftly moving rivers. Consider the following when crossing a river:

Meanders

Find where the river begins to expand, as the water current typically slows here sediment and rock accumulations will create an elevated area that is easier to pass over, this section will still appear a bit unruly compared to the calmest section of the stream. The calmest section of a stream is generally the deepest part with the least amount of traction and potential for quicksand.

Volume

Plan your day accordingly; river volumes and currents tend to increase as the day progresses.

Depth

If you are unsure of the depth, assess if you can safely wade in the cars intended path, if the stream is uncrossable on foot you will not be able to cross in an unmodified 4x4.

Precipitation

If rain is on the forecast the day of your river crossing, currents and water volume can change in as quickly as 30 minutes.

Commit

Once you have selected a spot to cross, put your vehicle into four-wheel drive. Do not try to change gears while in the water. Change gears once you are back on dry land.

F ROAD OPENINGS

AVERAGE OPENING DATES OF PRINCIPAL MOUNTAIN ROADS.

F206 Lakagígar	F208 Fjallabaksleið nyrðri	F225 Landmannaleið Landmannalaugar	F550 Kaldidalur	F902 Kverkfjöll	F26 Sprengisandur	F35 Kjölur (Hveravellir)	F52 Uxahryggir	F88 Askja
JUNE 12th	**JUNE 12th**	**JUNE 15th**	**JUNE 13th**	**JUNE 19th**	**JUNE 27th**	**JUNE 11th**	**JUNE 5th**	**JUNE 20th**

RENTAL CAR COMPARISON BY PRICE

Option A - New Cars:
July 7th to 14th (7 days)

HERTZ
http://www.hertz.com
Toyota Aygo:	795,96€
Toyota Rav4:	1.698,9€

EUROPCAR
http://www.holdur.is/en
Hyundai I10:	747,4€
Suzuki Grand Vitara 4x4:	1.521,1€

REYKJAVÍK CARS
http://www.reykjavikcars.com
Hyundai i10:	535,3€
Suzuki Grand Vitara 4x4:	1.036€
(GPS Included FREE)	

AVIS
www.avis.is
Hyundai I10:	742€
Suzuki Grand Vitara 4x4:	1.688€

SIXT
http://www.sixt.com/
VW Polo:	736€
Dacia Duster 4x4:	1.434€

CARS ICELAND
http://www.carsiceland.com
Kia Rio Diesel:	555€
Dacia Duster 4x4:	1.078€

Option B - Old Cars:
July 7th to 14th (7 days)

REYKJAVÍK CARS
(old models)
http://www.reykjavikcars.com
Hyundai I10:	398,8€
Suzuki Jimny 4x4:	708€

SS CAR-RENTAL
http://www.carrentalss.com
Hyundai I10:	405,8€
Toyota Rav4 4x4:	944€

SADCARS
http://sadcars.com/en
Toyota Yaris:	482,34€
Toyota Rav4 4x4:	976,2€

CHEAP RENTAL CAR
http://www.cheapcarhireiceland.is/
Toyota Yaris:	469,34€
Ford Escape 4x4 Auto:	805,59€

ICELAND CAR RENTAL
http://www.icelandcarrental.is
Hyundai I10:	585,8€
Toyota Rav4:	1064,2€

GEYSIR
http://www.geysir.is
Hyundai I10:	514,8€
Honda CRV 4x4:	1132,2€

PACKING FOR ICELANDIC WEATHER CONDITIONS AND TERRAIN

BECAUSE ICELAND SITS IN THE PATH OF THE Irminger Current and receives a steady circulation of warm air fed by the North Atlantic Drift, the climate tends to be more temperate, particularly in the region of the capital where the current has been swept westward from the southern coast. Cool summers transition into moderately cold and windy winters, with snowfall accumulating predominately at higher and more northern latitudes. Different regions of the island can vary greatly in temperature, precipitation and especially wind speed. While the south coast and the highlands typically receive the brunt of the wind force, various topographical anomalies can create a change in wide direction and create strong currents in the low lying areas of the country. Loose ash and fine particle debris, coupled with strong glacial winds result in heavy dust storms in the early summer highlands are in the vicinity of the Vatnajökull glacier. While thunderstorms are quite rare in Iceland, rainstorms are aplenty thanks to the Gulf Stream sweeping over the south coast. No matter the season, always be prepared to brave the rain, especially since it always seems to be raining on some part of the Ring Road.

Icelander's have a saying:

"THERE IS NO SUCH THING AS BAD WEATHER, JUST BAD CLOTHING"

THE LIST

Outerwear: Water resistant and waterproof outerwear is an absolute necessity, no matter the season in Iceland. It is a bonus if your outerwear happens to be windproof as well. Do not fret however if your shell is not also a windbreaker, enough layers will keep the wind from penetrating.

Sunglasses: These are an absolute necessity, and will undoubtedly make your glacial hike on a highly reflective surface that much more pleasant. They are also particularly useful when driving long distances in sun-illuminated valleys.

Photo Equipment: Bring a sufficient amount of memory cards and batteries. In addition, to being difficult to procure in small villages, the price of such luxury commodities is exorbitant in Iceland.

Shoes: If you plan on deviating from the main walking path, shoes with ankle support are a must. Terrain in Iceland is uneven and rough, with the highlands being particularly jagged. If you plan on doing any of the guided glacial hikes you may be forced to rent a pair of shoes, if your own shoes aren't deemed to have enough ankle support for the trek. With medical services often being miles removed from many points of interest, a twisted ankle can wreak havoc on your trip.

Eye Mask & Earplugs: Waking up to daylight at 3am is very disorienting, especially if the locals are still partying.

Hair conditioner: The mineral content of geothermal water leaves hair unmanageable, but otherwise undamaged.

Socks: A good pair of socks may make as big of a difference as good pair of shoes. Consider getting lightweight, moisture-wicking socks for the warmer season, and investing in mountaineering socks for warmth and cushioning in the winter. If you find that your feet blister no matter the shoes or socks you wear, I recommend packing a few blister band-aids; they really speed up the healing process. A friction block stick will also prevent any further chafing.

Medications: It can be quite difficult to find medication for the common cold in Iceland. If you feel something coming on prior to the departure of your trip, pack nasal spray and an over the counter cold medication. Many of the pharmacies in Iceland do not carry Day/Nyquil, Sudafed, Robitussin, ect. If you suffer from motion sickness and plan on whale watching, island hopping, or sea-angling, be sure to pack motion sickness pills.

Ski Pants: unless you plan on skiing you will not need ski pants. It is however, a good idea to pack water resistant bottoms for glacial hikes and winter trips,

First Aid: With an abundance of lava rock every which way, it is easy to scrape or cut yourself. Be sure to bring, at the very minimum, antibacterial ointment and some bandaging materials.

Documents: Driver's License and Passport, especially if you are renting a car.

Map: Buy a good map of Iceland, or invest in a rent-a-GPS through any Icelandic car rental agency.

Food:

If you are traveling on a tight budget, consider packing granola, cereal bars, dried fruit, and nuts. These will often cost much more in Iceland. Purchasing a yogurt and pouring in your own toppings makes an instant breakfast wherever you are.

Thermals: A thermal top will be of significant use in the wintertime.

Baby wipes:

It may sound strange, especially if you do not have children, but moist wipes are invaluable. Wipe the sulfur dust from your shoes and jacket shell. Clean your hands after a long hike or freshen up if there is no water to be had.

Sun Protection:

There is very little shade in Iceland, and it is possible to get sunburned even on overcast days.

Accessories: If you are going to be in Iceland between September and April, pack a pair of gloves and a well-insulated hat. Balaclavas offer invaluble protection from the elements.

A Bathing Suit:

This may be of use year-round, as hot tubs and geothermal pools are accessible no matter the season.

Towel:

Unless your accomodation provides you with one, it is useful to bring a small towel. You never know when you'll stumble upon naturally occurring geothermal hot spots in your sightseeing adventures. On occasions such as this, it will be nice to have towel to dry off with.

GETTING INTO
ICELAND

Flying: Flights into Iceland take approximately 5 to 6 hours from the East Coast of the United Sates. However, flights from Western Europe take only 3 to 4 hours.

Passports and Visas: Many visitors from Western nations do not require a visa for entry. If you are visiting from a country under the Schengen Agreement, you only need a recognized ID card. Visitors from the United Sates, the United Kingdom, Canada, and Australia, require a passport with a validity of at least three months beyond your intended stay. For further information visit www.utl.is

Liquid Limitations: Each individual liquids container may not exceed 100ml or 3.4fl oz. All liquids, aresols, and gels must be stowed in one transparent and re-selable plastic bag whose capacity does not exceed 1 liter. The combined volume of all liquids must also not exceed 1 liter.

Alcohol: may be purchased at the duty free shop in the arrival hall of Keflavík Airport at a significantly lower cost than any other establishments in Iceland.

Tax and VAT Refunds:
In Iceland, a 25.5% VAT is applied to most goods and services. A reduced VAT of 7% is applied to accomodations, literary and music materials, hot water, electricity and oil for heating houses, in addition to food (but not alcoholic beverages), and toll fees. Non-citizens are deemed eligible for a refund if the total value of goods exceeds ISK 4,000, and is to be taken out of the country within three months of purchase. If you are making large purchases ask for a tax free form, which is available at most buisness establishments. The proprietor of the shop will fill out the form for you. Be certain that the form is signed, and that the recipt for your purchases is attached. VAT refund booths are located the Keflavík Airport, Seyðisfjörður ferry terminal, the Reykjavík Tourist Center, and inside of Reykjavík malls.

Car Ren

Pick

Keflavík

International Airport

Scheduled Buses

Air Terminal

P1 Departures

P2 Arrivals

Taxi

Drop-off

P3 Long Term Parking

P Staff Parking

- Short Term Parking (Paid)
- Long Term Parking (Paid)
- Car Rentals
- Buses
- Taxi's
- Air Terminal
- Walkway
- Roads

To/From Reykjavík →

GETTING INTO
REYKJAVÍK

GETTING INTO THE CAPITAL CITY OF REYKJAVÍK from Keflavík Airport is as simple and straightforward as much of the upcoming journey around the Ring Road. Although new and clean, the airport is small and compact; you will not have to concern yourself with rushing around in order to catch connecting transportation. The city itself is the largest populated area on the island, with a little over 120,000 inhabitants residing in the city and far reaching suburbs. Nevertheless, it is entirely possible to navigate the city center on foot, or bicycle if you so desire.

To reach Reykjavík you have four options:

a.   The Flybus is a bus service that runs in conjunction with incoming and outgoing flights. It departs 35-40 minutes after each arriving flight from a station located outside the terminal building. If your flight is delayed, the bus will be as well. The trip takes about 45 minutes one way, and tickets may be purchased online or at the airport at cost of €12.50 per person, with discounts on child and roundtrip tickets. For a list of accommodations that offer Flybus pick-ups, and any other additional information, such as timetables and advanced booking, consult www.re.is/flybus/

b.   Gray Line Airport Express is another 24-hour bus service that runs in conjunction with all Keflavík's flights. Transfers take about 45 minutes, and buses depart from the airport terminal 30-40 minutes after each arriving flight. One-way tickets coast a little over €15. To book your transfer, visit www.airportexpress.is/

c.   Taxi: Rides from Keflavík International Airport cost about €85 for 1-4 passengers, and €110 for 5-8 passengers. A cost comparison between eight taxi cab services listed on the airport's website reveals City-Taxi to be the best deal for 1-4 passengers, while Taxi- Reykjavík is a slightly better deal for 5-8 passengers.

d.   Rental Car: While a rental car is not the most cost effective solution, depending on the season, it may be cheaper by the day than one taxi ride from the airport. If your plan is to do either the circumference of the Ring Road, or just the Golden Circle, renting a car in most cases is more accommodating and cheaper than taking several bus tours.

Tip: When inspecting your rental car be sure to dip down and inspect the undercarriage of the vehicle for any noticeable damage. It may seem silly, but lest you want to be held responsible for a previous drivers damage, you'll come away with an extra piece of mind. You don't have to be a car person to know what to look for, if something is severely damaged, it should be discernible.

Driving to Reykjavík with your rental car:
The drive from the airport into the Reykjavík is approximately 50 km, or 40 minutes along route 41 and then route 40 if you are heading into the city center. All of the roads and highways are extremely well-labeled throughout the entire island, and make navigation very driver friendly.

GETTING AROUND

Reykjavík

Once you are in Reykjavík and have situated yourself in your accommodations, the day is your oyster. The city center has a top-notch pedestrian footpath, and many of the sights are located within a few streets of one another.

Public Transportation: If you would like to utilize the Strætó, Reykjavík's public bus system, a single ride will cost you 350 kr. You will need to provide the driver with the exact amount, as he or she absolutely cannot give change back. If you require a transfer to reach your destination, ask the driver for an exchange ticket, which will provide you with another 75 minutes of travel time. Please note that city buses cease operation around 11pm.

By car: Any local will tell you that navigating the city by car is the preferred mode of transportation, and for a city that has the most cars per capita in the world, there is a surprising amount of parking available. Parking in the city center more than likely means that you'll be feeding the meter around 100kr per hour. Thanks to technologically advanced meters you may pay the amount with a credit card. Note that many of the streets in the center are one-way, in most cases this will be indicated by a sign, or by noting the direction of parked cars.

DAY 1 ITINERARY

BREAKFAST IN REYKJAVÍK
EXPLORE REYKJAVÍK CITY CENTER (SEE HALLGRÍMSKIRKJA AND LAUGAVEGUR)
LUNCH IN REYKJAVÍK, OR AT THE BLUE LAGOON
BLUE LAGOON
KRÝSUVÍK-SELTÚN GEOTHERMAL FIELDS
SELATANGAR RUINS
DINNER IN REYKJAVÍK
STROLL THROUGH THE OLD HARBOR

Personal Experience: Even with a yearning desire to hit the road immediately upon arriving in Iceland, I had to resist this rather ambitious endeavor. While our flight arrived early enough for us to have breakfast, and burn some petrol out on the Ring Road all before noon, I felt unable to devote my undivided attention to any important sights. As a photographer, I felt that I needed a day to recharge from all of the flying; and as a tourist, I wanted this to be a relaxing spa and city exploration day. Rightly so it was, the contrast of sensations between the cold raindrops and the warm lagoon water made the experience feel ethereal.

Exploring Reykjavík's city center on foot is one of the best ways to go. If you are driving your car into the city from your accommodation, there are a variety of parking options available to you. Choose from one of the many multi-storey car parks, pay-and-display zones, meters, or simply cruise about until you spy a free spot in the nearby residential areas. Just remember that the closer you park to the center the more expensive it will be. Parking meters and ticket dispensers accept both Icelandic coins and credit cards. Once parked, head to Skólavörðustígur hill. There, you will be greeted by the sight of a Leifur Eiríksson statue before the tallest church in Iceland, the incredibly modern Hallgrímskirkja church. Upon concluding your visit to the Lutheran church, make your way to Laugavegur, one of Iceland's oldest merchant streets. The name of this street literally means "wash road." Reykjavík's first settlers once used this route to reach the hot springs where all of the laundry was washed by hand. Today, you will find a variety of boutiques, dining establishments, galleries, and more.

After exploring the city to your heart's content, head off to the Blue Lagoon for a relaxing dip in the warm mineral-rich waters. The drive to the Lagoon from the city center is 47km or fifty minutes by car. Take route 40, which gradually turns into route 41. A the roundabout, take the 1st exit onto Route 43. On the final stretch of Route 43 take a right and then a left to reach the spa. The steam from the thermal baths is visible from the road.

To reach the next destination from the Blue Lagoon, head northwest to return back to route 43 and take a right, drive until you can make a right onto route 425; the Krýsuvík-Seltún geothermal fields will be on the left.

Next stop, the abandoned fishing village known as the Selatangar ruins. Head north on Route 425, making a right onto Route 43, then turn left onto Ránargata. From here, take the 1st left onto Austurvegur, and continue onto Route 427, taking a slight left to stay on Route 427 and then turn right; the ruins will be on the left. To head back to Reykjavík for dinner and an evening stroll, head north and take a right onto route 427. From here, turn left onto route 42, and follow until making a right onto route 41, which will eventually turn back into route 40, leading you to the city.

DAY 2 – THE GOLDEN CIRCLE
BREAKFAST IN REYKJAVÍK
ÞINGVELLIR NATIONAL PARK
GEYSIR
LUNCH
GULLFOSS
DINNER IN HVERAGERÐI

To head for the Golden Circle, take the Ring Road (Route 1) going north out of Reykjavík. After driving through the town of Mosfellsbær take the first exit on the right at the roundabout onto route 36 to Þingvellir. On the approach to the national park on route 36 you will see the barren landscape give way to rich and thick moss beds. At one point, you will see a host of small and large cairns, rock towers built predominantly by tourists. From here, the first view of Lake Þingvallavatn becomes visible in the distance.

While this sight of seemingly endless rock structures is truly something to behold on the vastly flat and seemingly inhospitable landscape, the building of cairns on public or park land is illegal in Iceland. The reason being is that legitimately built cairns are often used to point to the continuing direction of a hiking trail, and tampering with, or building additional structures has gotten people lost. Moreover, removing rocks for their original site leaves the slow to recover landscape marred holes that fill with water.

To reach the Geysir from Þingvellir National Park, head southeast on route 36. From here, continue onto route 365. At the roundabout, take the second exit onto Laugarvatnsvegur/route 37, and continue onto route 35. There is ample parking available at the gift shop and restaurant just across the street from the sights. If you opt to have lunch at the neighboring Hótel Geysir Restaurant, there is a buffet served each day from 11:30am – 2pm, with international and Icelandic fare. To view the menu visit: www.geysircenter.is/ and click on Restaurant/Lunch Buffet

The Gullfoss is just a short 10km drive from the Geysir, along route 35. To drive back into town, head south taking road 35 back to the Ring Road to reach Hveragerði (gps coordinates 64°0'0" N, 21°12'0" W). To view the menu for Café Gullfoss, visit www.gullfoss.is/cafe/

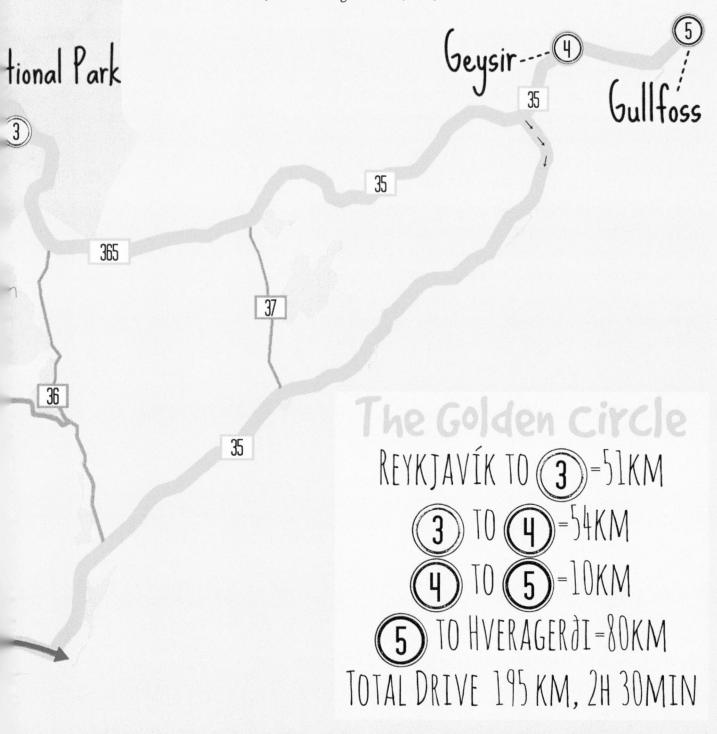

The Golden circle

REYKJAVÍK TO ③ = 51KM

③ TO ④ = 54KM

④ TO ⑤ = 10KM

⑤ TO HVERAGERÐI = 80KM

TOTAL DRIVE 195 KM, 2H 30MIN

DAY 3 ITINERARY

(2X2 ROUTE, OPTION 2)
BREAKFAST IN HVERAGERÐI
HVERAGERÐI GEOTHERMAL PARK
HIKE TO REYKJADALUR "SMOKE VALLEY"
LUNCH IN HVERAGERÐI
SELJALANDSFOSS
SKÓGAFOSS
DINNER IN VÍK

Following breakfast in Hveragerði, head for the center of this scenic town to explore the Geothermal Park in which mud pots boil, food is cooked, and spa treatments are available. At the conclusion of your visit, head to the Reykjadalur valley for few hours of serene hiking. To reach the parking lot that marks the beginning of the trailhead, drive north on the main street, Breiðamörk, which slowly ascends into the surrounding Hengill Mountains. On the route, there will be a slight division in the road; keep left for the road to Reykjadalur. This is your destination and the end of any drivable road. Cross the small bridge over the Varmá River to reach the trailhead for the area. Take the ascending Rjúpnabrekkur trail, which will eventually lead you into the Reykjadalur valley, first passing several active mud pools and a stream crossing. The bathing destination is apparent when a camping hut becomes visible to the east, where a cold stream passes. Note that the hot stream passes to the west, and the place that the two streams meet is the ideal place to bathe and relax.

Return to Hveragerði for lunch taking the same route back.
To make the hour long drive to Seljalandsfoss head out on the Ring Road and eventually make a left onto route 249; the waterfall will be on the right. Note that the F-249 road that winds around Eyjafjallajökull is only for 4x4 vehicles. Continue to Skógafoss by travelling along the Ring Road for 27km until you can make a left onto Skógar, and then the first left for Skógafoss.

The small village of Vík í Mýrdal is situated directly along the Ring Road. To reach this destination take a left onto the Ring Road from Skógar; its 33km away.

F225

26

F208

Hekla ⑥

Landmannalaugar ⑦

F208

208

Eyjafjallajökull

F249 ⑧

249

⑨

--Seljalandsfoss

⑨

Skógafoss--

Vik

⑩

1

OPTION 1

OPTION 2

Day 3 Itinerary

(4X4 Route during High Season, Option 1)

Breakfast in Hveragerði
Head to Hekla
Hiking in Landmannalaugar
Dinner in Landmannalaugar Head
to Vík in the morning

Hveragerði

1

Scenario: Depending on the type of vehicle you have rented and the amount of time you have, you may be able to spring for both of the options listed for day three. If you have a 4x4, and would like to do both of the itineraries during the course of two separate days (it is impossible to do both in the same day) you may proceed with the routes clockwise or counter-clockwise. Either way is sure to cover some of the same ground twice. If you have a 4x4, and are wondering if it is worth your time to drive back along the 2x2 route, the answer is yes; both of the waterfalls featured are some of the most beautiful Iceland has to offer. If you are thinking about renting a 2x2, and are wondering if you should get a 4x4 so that you may take the F-roads as well, consider your fitness level. All of the major sights in Iceland are for the most part accessible via 2x2, however, if you love to hike and climb, some of the best routes will be along the F-roads.

Keep in mind that most inland F-roads are only open in the high season. To reach option two's destinations, head out onto the Ring Road after a breakfast in Hveragerði. Follow the Ring Ring road until you can turn onto route 26. From here, go 49km to reach route F-225, and approximately another 7km to reach the pointing sign that reads "Hekla." The road will become rougher at this junction, as it leads to the last tier parking lot at the beginning of Hekla's trailhead. You can opt to meet your hired guide here, or venture onto the relatively well-marked trail at your own risk. You can obtain mountain conditions, or hire a guide at the nearby farm/hotel Leirubakki. For more information visit: www.leirubakki.is

If you continue alongF-225, it will eventually turn into F-208 after you ford a river. Yes, the river is a full sized river. It is not a cakewalk even during the high season, but with tremendous care, knowledge, and a good 4x4 vehicle, it is passable on a good day. A "good day" in Iceland depends on the prior day's weather. If there has been a great deal of rain in the area, I'm afraid to say that it will be a waste of time to attempt this route unless you are in a modified 4x4, snorkel and all. It is possible to pass the river on foot via a footbridge, with a trail continuing onto Landmannalaugar. There is a car park before the river where you may leave your vehicle. However you will have to carry your supply from here on out. Note that there is one accommodation available in Landmannalaugar, and should be booked well in advance, at www.fi.is/en/huts/ (click on the Landmannalaugar Hut). Camping is always an option, and showers are available at a small cost to campers at the premises of the hut. To reach Vík in the morning, head along F-208 until it turns into route 208, eventually meeting up with the Ring Road. The drive will take approximately 3 hours, and you will have to ford several wide streams.

F225

26

Hekla ⑥

⑦ Landmannalaugar

F208

208

Eyjafjallajökull

F249 ⑧

249

⑨

--Seljalandsfoss

⑨

Skógafoss

Vik

1

⑩

OPTION 1

OPTION 2

DAY 4 ITINERARY

(2X2 ROUTE)

BREAKFAST IN VÍK

GLACIER CLIMBING IN VATNAJÖKULL
NATIONAL PARK

EAT LUNCH AT SKAFTAFELL VISITOR'S
CENTER CAFÉ

JÖKULSÁRLÓN LAKE

DINNER IN HÖFN

Note: This route requires advanced booking with a Glacier
Mountain Guide.

After breakfast, set course on the 1.5 hour long journey along
the Ring Road to the Skaftafell Visitor Centre in Vatnajökull
National Park. The center is located on the left hand side on
road 998. Here you will check in with your mountain guide
and be outfitted with the proper gear for your hike. Following
your glacial adventures head back to the Ring Road for a 56km
drive to the glacial lake, Jökulsárlón. For the best viewing
areas, disregard the first parking lot you see, and opt instead
for the second parking lot located directly over the bridge. The
drive to the small town of Höfn is an hour along route 1, and a
deviation onto route 99, also know as Hafnavegur.

Va

Skaftafell Visit

1

Vik

jökull National Park

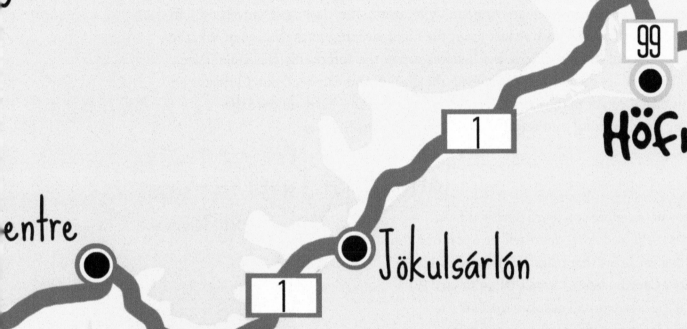

entre

Jökulsárlón

1

99

Höfn

OPTIONAL DAY 4 ITINERARY
(4X4 ROUTE HIGH SEASON)
BRUNCH IN VÍK
HAMRAGARÐAHEIÐI
HIKING IN EYJAFJALLAJÖKULL AREA
DINNER IN VÍK

Whether you are just arriving in Vík from the last 4x4 adventure in Landmannalaugar or you've just spent the night sleeping in the village of Vík, the next optional itinerary for a 4x4 involves a trip the remote Eyjafjallajökull area. Unless you are hiring a guide to climb the glacier, you can head out a bit later on this day, if you need the extra sleep. When you are ready, head out onto the Ring Road, making your way to route 249 and eventually F-249.

However, before you reach the F-road (past Seljalandsfoss), there will be a pointing sign along route 249 that reads Hamragarðaheiði (GPS Coordinates: 63°37'36.4" N, 19°58'54.5" W). Take this scenic and desolate road until it runs at the top of the hill, here you will find either a beautiful view of the distant rock islands, or a dense fog that sits atop of a mystic moss bed.

Markarfljót River

F249

248

249

1

246

1

As you descend down from the top of the hill pull over for a views of the waterfall that runs through a deep and long crag. Now continue on your way to Eyjafjallajökull. The same way you came will be the same way you leave to return to Vík for the evening. The F-249 should not be taken lightly. There are as many as twelve rivulets running through the route on a good day. Once again, this type of terrain should only be tackled if good weather has preceded the trip. This area is known for its inhospitable landscape and serene desolation, there are no grand views to be had or major sights to behold. Make this trip if you have the time, and desire to simply enjoy the experience and the hiking.

Þórsmörk
National Park

Krossá River Crossing

F249

F249

Gígjökull

Katla

Eyjafjallajökull
Glacier

Mýrdalsjökull
Glacier

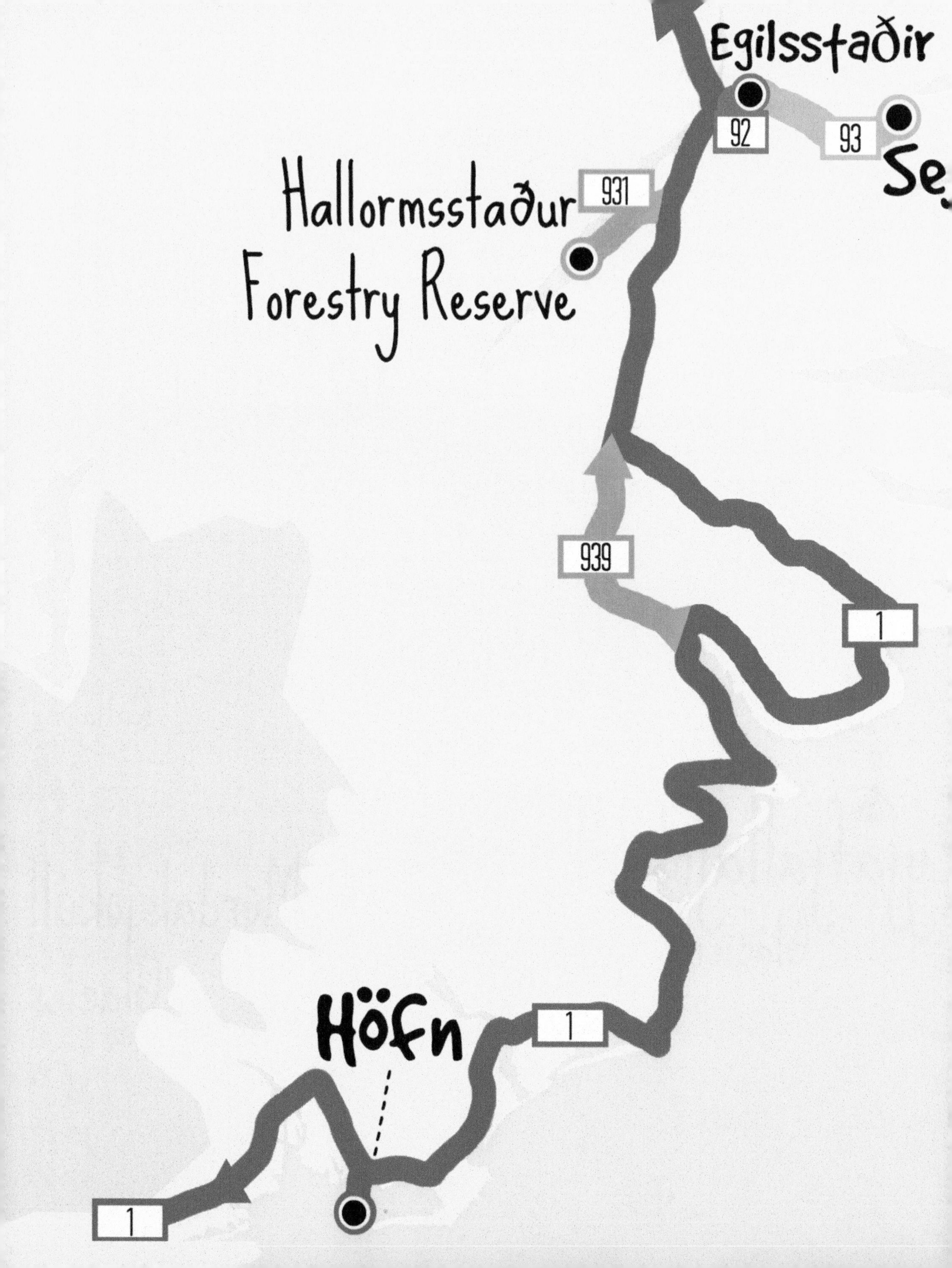

Egilsstaðir

92

93

Se

Hallormsstaður
Forestry Reserve

931

939

1

Höfn

1

1

sfjörður

While the past five days of the itinerary have been jam packed with all of the well-known sights of south Iceland, this drive into the northeast is delightfully refreshing. Along this route, trees will finally come into view on the rugged mountain terrain, due to the country's large reforestation movement. Note how many of the farms sitting in the steep boulder filled valleys have planted a wall of trees to protect their homes and livestock from the loose rock that tumbles down the steep mountainsides each spring thaw.

This route may not have any big name attractions attached to it but the drive is still nothing short of breath taking.

In the morning, set out for a relaxing hike around the glacial lake Logurinn, in Iceland's largest forest, Hallormsstaður. To reach the forest you can either drive along the Ring Road until you make a slight righ onto 931, or you can take a shortcut in the form of the 939 road to arrive faster.

If you visit the forest's website at http://www.hallormsstadur.is, you will find information about events and activities, such as boat and horse rentals.

Egilsstaðir, is 24km from the Hallormsstaður Forest. When you are ready to head there for lunch, take route 931 (heading north) to return to the Ring Road. From here, the town will be another 11km away on route 92. It is a good idea to fuel up and check your tire pressure at a gas station here before heading out on the mountain road.

The drive to Seyðisfjörður should be made while there is still a sufficient amount of daylight as the mountain road can be a bit daunting even though it is fully paved. Nevertheless, the drive is well worth it, and there are no words to explain the beauty of gleaming mountain tops beneath a brilliant blue sky, and a road so desolate that less than a handful of cars will pass you on this drive. Seyðisfjörður cannot be missed, as the 93 drives directly through it. You will be able to see the small town come into view as you begin your descent down hill. There is a small dirt pull off for photography, but it is easy to miss if you are not anticipating it; look for a memorial statue on the passenger side of the road.

Day 6 Itinerary

Breakfast in Seyðisfjörður
Dettifoss
Krafla
Mývatn Nature Reserve
Dinner in Mývatn

The itinerary for this day takes you to the Mývatn Lake region, a popular tourist area in the north of Iceland, which features a plethora of activities, including hiking, sightseeing, and bathing. The first stop in what is likely to be an eventful day is Dettifoss, one of the largest and most powerful waterfalls in Europe. After breakfast, take one last look from the crest of the mountain at the little town in the valley, Seyðisfjörður. Upon returning to the Ring Road, drive about 130 km toward the Mývatn Lake region. Turn right onto route 864 towards Dettifoss, and drive approximately 30 km to reach a parking area, which is only a short hike from the falls. The falls are fed by the Vatnajökull glacier, and are quite an amazing splendor, but take care, because there are no railings to separate you and the falls, and the rocks may be quite slippery. When you are finished, head back to the Ring Road, and drive about 30 km to get to the Hverirgeothermal area. There is a parking area off to the left, but you will certainly smell it before you see it. The area is host to a number of mudpots, and fumaroles. The area has some great hiking, if you can bear the smell. An optional excursion is to the Krafla caldera, an active volcano, and the Viti crater, both of which are close to the geothermal area. Although not presently erupting, the area has some great lava formations, and makes for half a day's worth of hiking.

Seyðisfjörður

1

93

The road leading to Krafla is across the street from the geothermal area, and is about 8 km long, though you will have to park and hike into the formations.

Get back onto the Ring Road, and drive toward Mývatn Lake. Turn left onto route 848, and drive about 4 km to get to the Hverfjall crater. The access road is on the left, but the crater is easily seen from the road. Park, and hike up the crater for some great views of the entire Mývatn area.

After a full day of hiking, relax in one of the many hot springs around the lake. For details on hot springs in the area, visit http://jardbodin.is/en/.

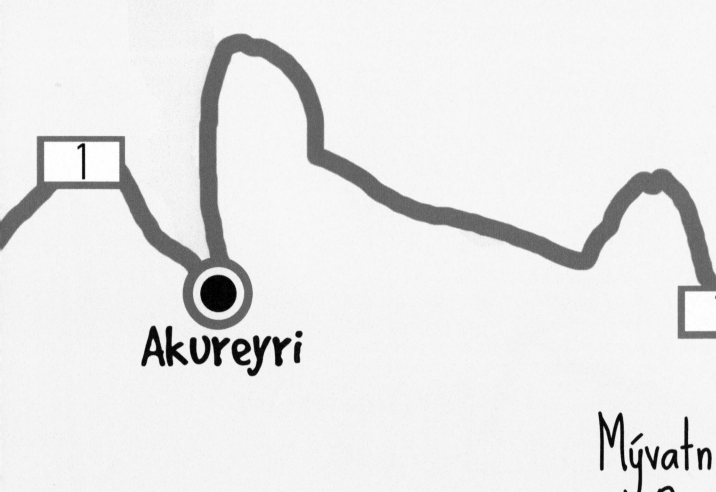

1

Akureyri

Mývatn
Rese

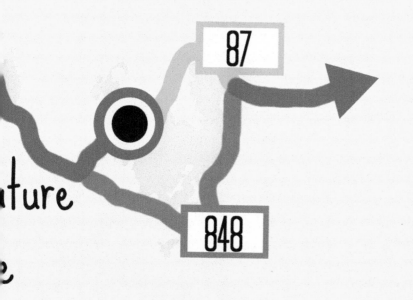

87

848

ature
e

DAY 7
ITINERARY
BREAKFAST IN MÝVATN
WHALE WATCHING IN AKUREYRI
LUNCH IN AKUREYRI
DINNER IN AKUREYRI

The Ring Road will take you directly from the Mývatn Nature Reserve to Akureyri. The drive time is 1h 10m, 90km.

Whale watching tours depart from Akureyri's Torfunesbryggja harbor, located in the town center down from the main church. The Ambassador offers three hour long tours, two to three times a day beginning in May and running through mid-October.

Adult Ticket Prices are ISK 9,990, with a 50% discount on children's tickets.

For booking information, and tour timetables visit: http://ambassador.is/

Be sure to check out the lively bar scene around the main square in Akureyri. The nightlife here is just as abundant and bustling as it is in the capital city of Reykjavík, if not more so. The northerners certaily know how to party, and the establishments are just as metropolitan as many of the establishments found in much larger European cities.

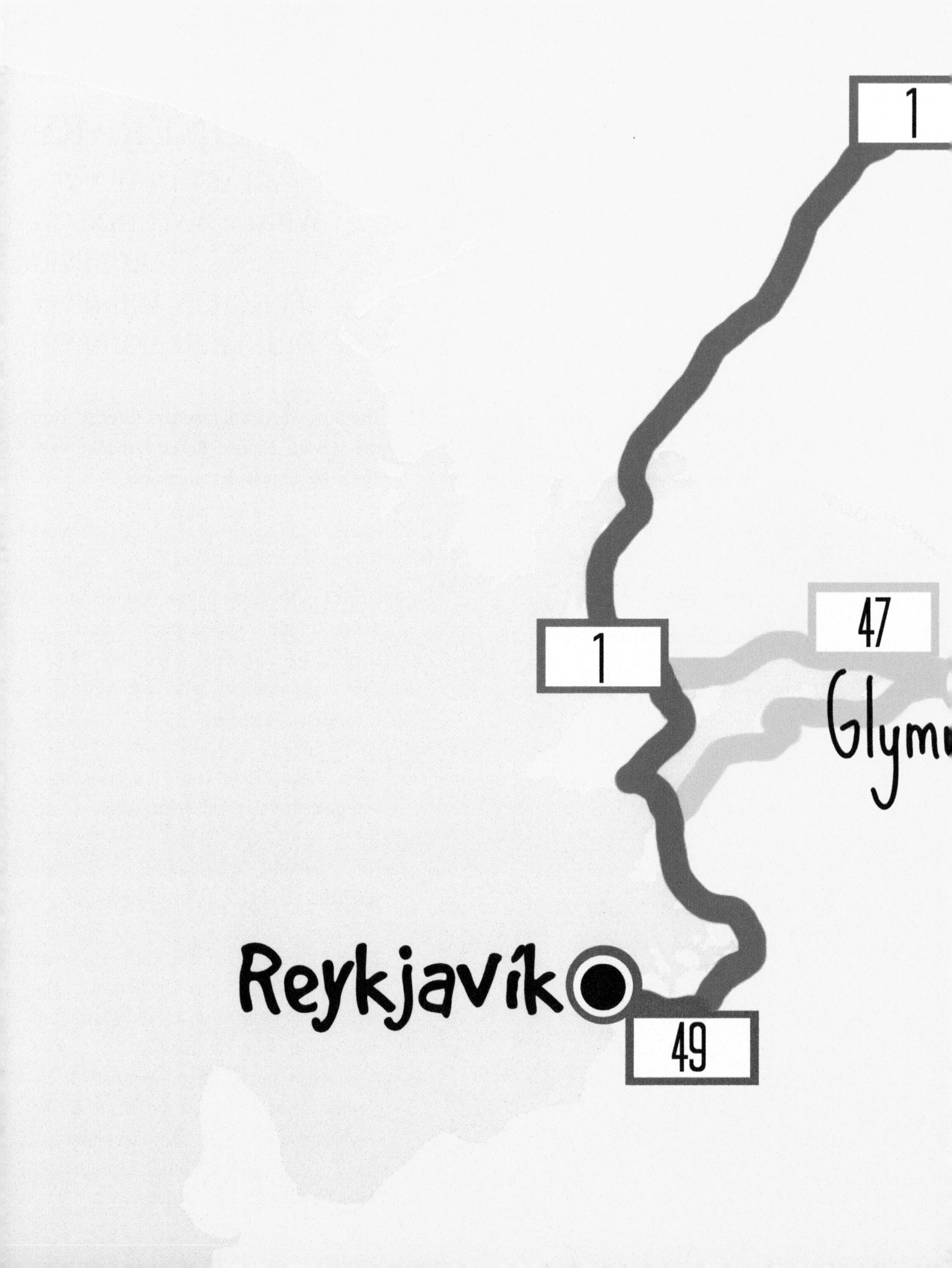
1
1
47
Glym
Reykjavík
49

DAY 8 ITINERARY
BREAKFAST IN AKUREYRI
GLYMUR OR TUNNEL
LUNCH AND DINNER IN REYKJAVÍK

To return to the capital city of Reykjavík, travel along the Ring Road for 314km, taking the second exit on the roundabout for Hvalfjarðargöng. The Hvalfjörður Tunnel is 5,770 meters in length and runs beneath the Hvalfjörður fjord, reaching a depth of 165 meters below sea level. It is presently the shortest distance connecting the western part of the island to northern cities like Akureyri, and reduces an hour-long drive to less than ten minutes. The present toll-rate for this tunnel is ISK1.000, and can be paid with credit card or cash. Following your exit from the tunnel, continue your journey along the Ring Road for another 25km, merging onto Route 49 to conclude the last leg of your journey, another 7km.

To return to Reykjavík with a stop over at Glymur, head out on the Ring Road from Akureyri, and turn left onto road 47 (Hvalfjarðarvegur). Drive to the Botnsá river, which is at the end of the fjord. Turn left, and drive about 3km inland where you will find a parking lot. Put your hiking boots on because the parking lot is quite a ways away from the waterfall itself. There are two main paths, one walking along the west bank of the river, and one along the east. Be preapared for a four-hour long, well-marked, round-trip hike. The eastern bank trail is the easier of the two, and provides for a better view of the falls. The trail is not for the faint of hear. It requires you to climb over rock formations and cross a shallow river bed before you reach Glymur. Once you return back to your car, follow route 47 to return back to the Ring Road.

Mountain Roads	Earliest Opening	Latest Opening	Median Opening
Lakagígar, F206	June 05	June 28	June 15
Fjallabaksleið nyrðri, F208			
a. Sigalda - Landmannalaugar	May 31	June 29	June 10
b. Laugar - Eldgjá	June 7	June 28	June 18
c. Eldgjá - Skaftártunga	May 31	June 10	June 08
Fjallabaksleið syðri, F210			
a. Keldur - Hvanngil	June 12	July 08	June 28
b. Hvanngil - Skaftártunga			
Landmannaleið, F225	June 02	July 05	July 14
Emstruleið, F261	June 12	July 01	July 24
Kjalvegur, 35			
a. Gullfoss - Hveravellir	June 05	June 22	June 12
b. Hveravellir - Blönduvirkjun	May 26	June 13	May 31
Sprengisandur, F26			
a. Hrauneyjar - Nýidalur	June 10	July 05	June 22
b. Nýidalur - Bárðardalur	June 23	July 13	July 03
Skagafjarðarleið, F752	June 30	July 13	July 05
Eyjafjarðarleið, F821	July 04	July 13	July 06
Öskjuvatnsvegur, F894	June 15	July 07	June 23
Vesturd, F862	June 03	June 25	June 05
Kverkfjalaleið, F902	June 14	June 24	June 19
Uxahryggjavegur, 52	April 24	May 31	May 12
Kaldadalsvegur, 550	June 05	June 29	June 14
Öskjuleið, F88			
a. Inn að Herðubreiðarlindum	June 14	July 24	June 21
b. Herðubreiðarlindir - Dreki	June 15	June 25	June 21

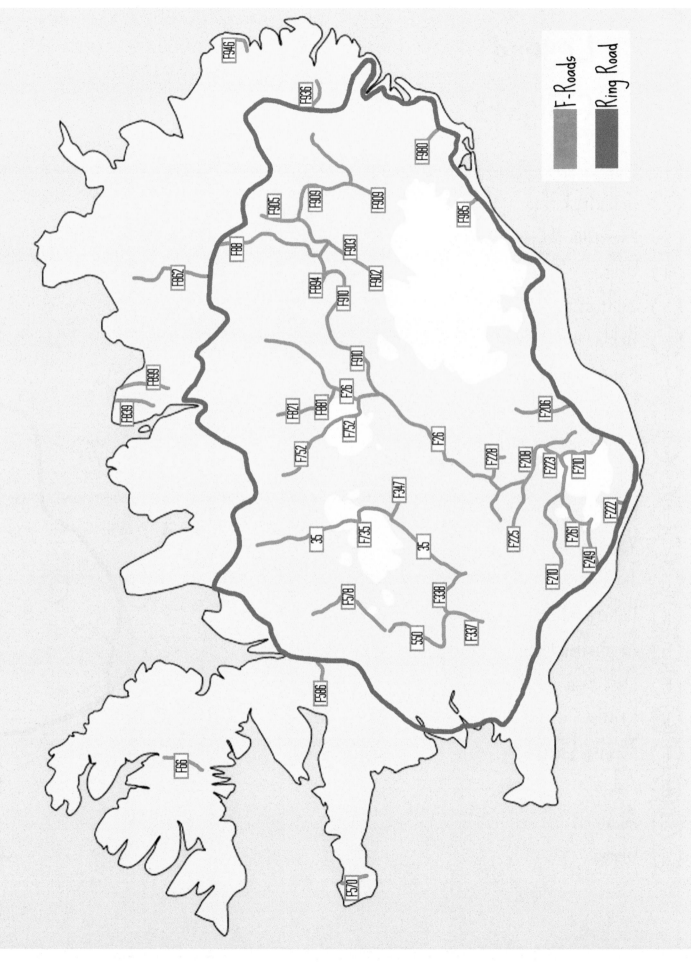

5

Legend
of Sights

1. Blue Lagoon
2. Hallgrímskirkja
3. Þingvellir National Park
4. Geysir
5. Gullfoss
6. Hekla
7. Landmannalaugar
8. Eyjafjallajökull
9. Seljalandsfoss and Skógafoss
10. Vik
11. Lakagígar
12. Vatnajökull National Park
13. Jökulsárlón
14. Hallormsstaður Forest
15. Seyðisfjörður
16. Dettifoss
17. Krafla
18. Mývatn Lake
19. Askja
20. Akureyri
21. Glymur

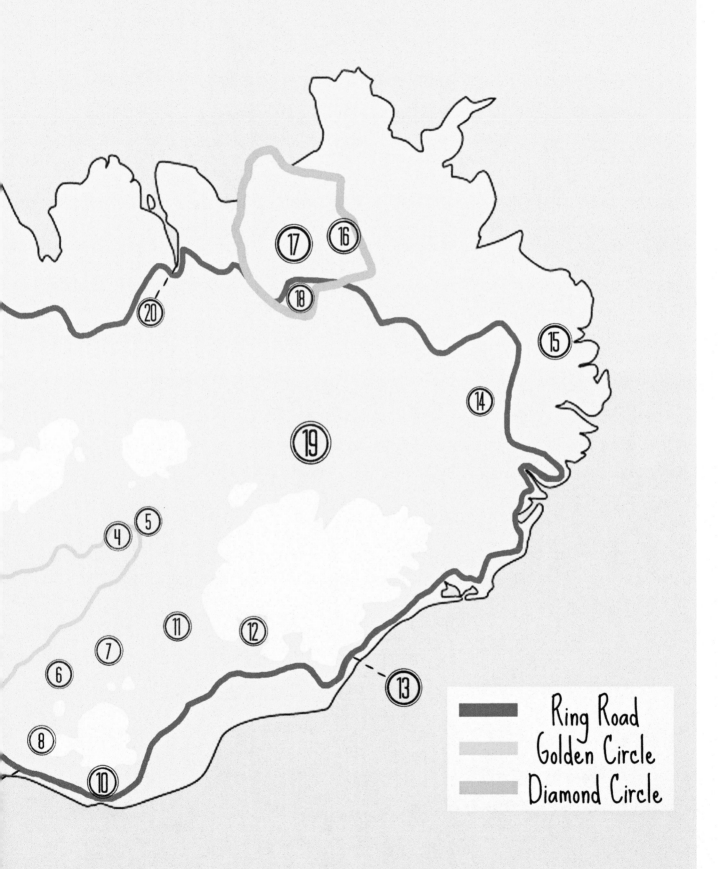

Ring Road
Golden Circle
Diamond Circle

This Lutheran parish church in Reykjavík, Iceland, designed to resemble the volcanic basalt columns visible in various areas of the island. Even though the design of the structure was first commissioned in 1937, construction of the church did not begin until 1954, and was finally completed 38 years later in 1992. The Hallgrímskirkja is located in the center of the city. It is the largest church in Iceland and one of the most well know manmade landmarks in the country. The church is named after poet and clergyman Hallgrímur Pétursson, and is home to a German built pipe organ, containing 5,275 pipes in total. The statue of Leifer Eriksson in the center courtyard of the church was a gift from the United States commemorating the 1000th anniversary of Iceland's Parliament at Þingvellir.

GPS Coordinates: 64°8'31" N, 21°55'39" W

Cost: Admission to the church is free

Photography: Take an elevator ride up the 75m tall tower for a breathtaking 360-degree view of the city. The cost is a little bit over 4 EUR for adults and a little bit over a euro for children, tickets are available for purchase at the church gift shop.

Do: If you are visiting between June and mid-August, you may hear the organ in concert on Sunday afternoons at 5 p.m., a cost of 10 EUR per person. Noon concerts are also available on varying days at lower cost. Consult http://www.listvinafelag.is/ for more information. If you cannot make it to a concert, a concert CD is available for sale at the church gift shop.

BLUE LAGOON

The Blue Lagoon first formed in 1976 as the water output from a nearby geothermal power plant collected in a large lava field. Within five years of its formation, the locals had discovered that the silica and sulfur rich water eased skin irritations related to psoriasis and acne. The Blue Lagoon bathing establishment was officially opened to the public in 1992, and is now open daily all year long. The lagoon sits 13 km from Keflavík International Airport and 39 km from Reykjavík, making it a great stopping or starting destination for any Icelandic adventure.

Hours of Operation: Hours vary from season to season, with peak times being from 10am to 2pm. If you are visiting during the high season book your tickets online and present the staff the staff with your confirmation code. To do this and more, visit http://www.bluelagoon.com/

Prices: Depending on the season, anticipate paying around 40 EUR per adult, and 20 EUR per teen for the standard package, which only includes entrance to the locker room and geothermal pools. Children thirteen years of age and younger are always free. Towels, bathrobes, and slippers, along with other services are available at additional costs. Your admittance to the pool will include an electronic wristband that will allow you to purchase refreshments and spa treatments that will be charged to your account upon exit.

GPS Coordinates:
63°52′48″ N, 22°26′53″ W

Baggage: The Blue Lagoon offers safe luggage storage at the Service Center in the main parking lot. The price is 3€ per bag. If you do not need to store your bags, continue past this first building down a narrow lava rock path to reach the main spa facility.

Food & Drink: There is a wide range of refreshments, light dining options, and even a gourmet restaurant on sight. Bringing your own food is always an option, but seating yourself at one of the dining areas to consume it is frowned upon. Eating in the parking lot may be the only way to consume your own food.

Facilities: The Blue Lagoon Clinic Hotel is a ten minutes walk from the Blue Lagoon, and admission to the geothermal pools is included in your room price. The hotel also offers its own private bathing lagoon, available only to guests at certain hours of the day.

Photography: If you are looking to photograph the blue lagoon you can enter the establishment just as you would if you were bathing. Within the lobby are several doors that lead out to the banks of the lagoon. If you walk into the adjoining restaurant, you can follow a staircase up to the roof for a panoramic view of the geothermal pools.

Miscellaneous: Your electronic wristband serves as your locker key in the changing room. Blow drying stations are set up around the perimeter of this area. If you are traveling in the company of the opposite sex, agree upon a meeting point in the lobby for your departure, since men's and women's facilities are on separate floors.

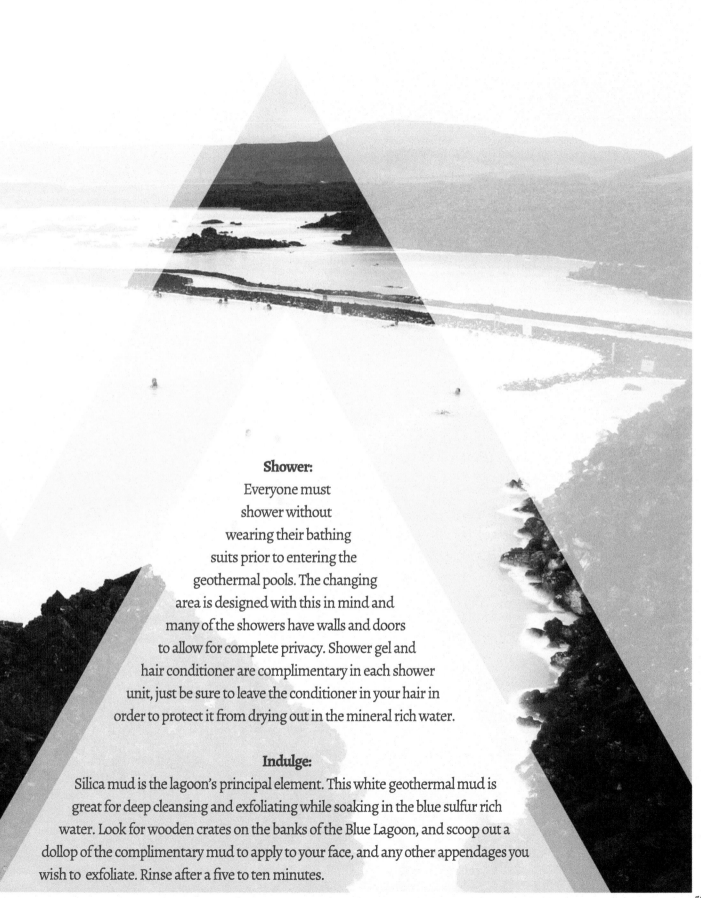

Shower:

Everyone must
shower without
wearing their bathing
suits prior to entering the
geothermal pools. The changing
area is designed with this in mind and
many of the showers have walls and doors
to allow for complete privacy. Shower gel and
hair conditioner are complimentary in each shower
unit, just be sure to leave the conditioner in your hair in
order to protect it from drying out in the mineral rich water.

Indulge:

Silica mud is the lagoon's principal element. This white geothermal mud is
great for deep cleansing and exfoliating while soaking in the blue sulfur rich
water. Look for wooden crates on the banks of the Blue Lagoon, and scoop out a
dollop of the complimentary mud to apply to your face, and any other appendages you
wish to exfoliate. Rinse after a five to ten minutes.

Hveragerði Geothermal Park:

The park is situated in the center of the geothermally powered town of Hveragerði. As you witness the underground vents blasting hot steam into the cool air, you will understand why the geothermal power made possible by the Hengill volcano is so interconnected with daily life for the people in this area. Park visitors are welcome to stroll through the marked footpaths, and learn about the geological happenings that make this town and its history unique.

GPS Coordinates:
64°00'04.6" N, 21°11'13.7" W

High Season Hours: Monday – Saturday, 9am - 6pm, Sunday, 10am - 4pm.

Do: For around 11€ per person you can soak your feet in the mud baths available at the park.

Eat: Consider purchasing a loaf of bread for sandwich making. Baked in the parks hot springs, they are sold at surrounding bakeries.

Krýsuvík-Seltún Geothermal Fields:

The Krýsuvík area consists of several geothermal fields situated on a fissure zone along the Mid-Atlantic Ridge, the most notable of which is Seltún. Here you may experience the same geological marvels that are found on a much larger scale in northeast Iceland. Follow the designated wooden path to see the vibrant colors of the soil, shaped by the surrounding fumaroles, mud pots, and hot springs. Be sure to cover your face, the smell of sulphur can be nauseating. Of the three lake-filled maars located near the fields, Grænavatn, Gestsstaðavatn, and Augun, Grænavatn is the most beautiful. Its vibrant and rich teal hue has formed from the presence of mineral deposits and thermal algae, so be sure to have your camera ready.

GPS Coordinates:
63°53'41.0"N, 22°03'05.4" W

The Reykjadalur "Smoke Valley"

This area derives its name from the steam that rises off of the soil from the plethora of steam vents, hot springs, and fumaroles that dot the Hengill volcanic region. The hike to Reykjadalur valley from the neighboring town of Hveragerði, has become popular in part due to a multitude of streams with varying temperatures accessible only on foot.

GPS Coordinates:
64°01'20.2" N, 21°12'41.1" W
(Parking lot at trailhead.)

Do: Bring your bathing suit on your hike. A map at the trailhead will illustrate which streams are the perfect temperatures for bathing. A roundtrip hike is approximately 6.5km.

Selatangar Ruins:

Long abandoned in the 1880's, this once industrious fishing village, home to some of Iceland's first settlers, is now a fleeting memory in the crags of the desolate and rocky landscape. All that remains are the stone foundations of the dwellings that were built right into the rugged terrain of this black lava field. Icelanders believe that the Selatangar ruins are home to the not so friendly Tanga-Tómas ghost, who was known to haunt the fishermen of long ago.

GPS Coordinates:
63°50'16.9" N, 22°14'26.5" W

Iceland's first national park,
founded in 1930, was established to protect the
meeting point of one of the world's oldest surviving national
parliaments, the Alþingi. The Alþingi, which was first founded in the
summer of 903, marked the beginning of the Icelandic Commonwealth, and
laid the groundwork for Iceland's national identity. The "Parliament Plains" are
located 45 km east of Reykjavík, with the general assembly eventually moving to its present
day establishment the Alþingishús in 1881. As of 2014 the Icelandic parliament celebrated 1111
years of existence, having had only one brief discontinuation of its meetings between 1799 to 1844.

Members of the first assembly meetings traveled from all regions of Iceland. The most difficult
and treacherous journeys belonged to the Eastern-most members, who had to navigate mountains and
glacial rivers for a total of 17 travel days to reach the Þingvellir region. In addition to Þingvellir being a
site of vast cultural heritage and historical importance, it also happens to be of great geological
value , as a rift valley in this region marks the crest of the Mid-Atlantic Ridge.

IONAL PARK

The Þingvellir National Park
is one of the most popular tourists
attractions within the boundaries of the
Golden Circle, and is filled with a multitude of
attractions. Some things at Þingvellir remain the
same, in the sense that this region remains as
much of a gathering place as it once was. So
in 1928, the park was decreed the perpetual
property of the Icelandic nation, and never to be
sold or leased.
In 2004 the national park was made a
Unesco World Heritage Site.

ÞINGVELLIR
THE GOLDEN CIRCLE

THE ÞINGVELLIR PARK VISITOR CENTER

is located on top of the Almannagjá fault, parallel to the footpath the leads down into the fault ridge. Admission to the park, the visitors center, and parking are all free. The visitor center is almost entirely electronic and interactive, with video and audio material being offered in Danish, English, German, French and Icelandic. The Visitor Centre is open daily, 9 a.m. - 5 p.m year round. Twenty-four hour restroom facilities are on the premise at the cost of 200 ISK, payable by card and cash. For more information about park activities, history, permits, and driving routes, visit http://www.thingvellir.is/english

GPS Coordinates: 64°15′29″ N, 21°7′30″ W

THE LÖGBERG (Law Rock) was the speaking platform and focal point of the "Parliament Plains." The elected law speaker that presided over all assemblies stood upon the Lögberg to recite the law of the land, before the law was written down. Law speakers, who were elected for a term of three years, recited the law and assembly procedures from memory each meeting. All rulings concerning the entire nation of Iceland where made by the Law Council, with the Lögberg as their platform, until it was stripped of its power by the Norwegian crown in 1271. The law rock continued to serve as a courtroom until 1798.

ÞINGVELLIR NATIONAL PARK is in quite a predicament. It neighbors the ridge where the North American and European continental plates are pulling apart from one another. The Reykjanes Ridge rises out of the Atlantic Ocean to the southwest of Iceland, and is part of the Mid-Atlantic Ridge. The parallel ridges that are left as a result of this divergent tectonic plate activity are very prominent surface features at the Þingvellir National Park. The average spreading rate for the Reykjanes Rige is 2.5 cm per year, and because this movement is not smooth, tectonic activity and earthquakes have been reported in the rift valley.

THE ALMANNAGJÁ GORGE marks the eastern boundary of the North American continental plate. The gorge is one of the few places you can walk along the Mid-Atlantic Ridge without it being submerged deep in the ocean. In 2011, a new fissure was discovered in the southern part of the gorge, and due to the tremendous depth and width, this section now has a bridge running over top.

ÖXARÁFOSS & ÖXARÁ RIVER is a tributary of Lake Þingvallavatn. As the water flows over the lip of the ridge, it forms the rocky Öxaráfoss waterfall, which is one of the main sights at the Þingvellir National Park.

ÞINGVALLAVATN is a rift valley lake, with an abundance of Arctic Charr, in Þingvellir national park. Its surface area makes it the largest natural lake on the island of Iceland. Because most of the water feeds into the lake through mineral rich lava fields, the lake is lush with vegetation even though the climate is cold. The most popular sights in the Þingvallavatn Lake are the Silfra and Davíðsgjá tectonic fissures.

Þingvallakir

ÞINGVALLAKIRKJA: The present and protected church building at Þingvellir dates from the 1850s, but sits on the site of a larger church dating back to the early 11th century when Christianity was first accepted. The original church was unfortunately destroyed in a storm in 1118, and has been rebuilt several times since. The present day church houses a collection of three bells of varying ages, one ancient, the second from 1697, and the third from 1944. Within the Þingvallakirkjugarður graveyard rest two Icelandic poets, Jónas Hallgrímsson (1807-1845) and Einar Benediktsson (1864-1940). Þingvallakirkja is open daily 9am to 5pm, from the middle of May to the beginning of September, with church services being held once a month.

Do: If you are scuba certified, dive into the pristine freshwater fissure, Silfra. If you are not certified, there is no need to miss out, snorkeling can be just as much of an adventure, and in fact can be a whole family affair. This unique geological phenomenon enables you to dive between two continental plates, and boasts several locations at which, with arms extended, you can touch both the North American and Eurasian plates at the same time. With crystal clear visibility upwards to 100 m an underwater camera is sure to capture an experience of a lifetime. Arrange for Þingvallavatn Lake related activities at http://www.dive.is/

Do:

Throw a coin into the Peningagjá (money vault), formerly known as the Nikulásargjá fault. This tradition began in 1907 after the fault was bridged for the visit of a Danish king. It is customary to watch your coin fall until you can see it no more for full wish fulfillment, at which point it will lay with a myriad of other coins sparkling on a sunny day in the crystal clear and deathly cold waters of the fissure. Please note to only throw money into this particular fissure.

GEYSIR: The ten thousand year old Geysir lies in the Haukadalur valley along with thirty much smaller geysers in the Golden Circle. Eruptions are infrequent, however, and have, in the past, ceased altogether for years at a time; such changes in patterns of eruption have been attributed to seismic activity. Particularly strong and frequent earthquakes in the valley lead to the openings of several more geysers in 1294. In 1896, a strong earthquake revived the Geysir after a long period of dormancy, but in 1916 activity ceased once more. In June 2000, an earthquake of 6.5 magnitude on the Richter scale hit the Haukadalur area, making the Great Geysir erupt sporadically once more.

STROKKUR is one of the most famous geysers in the Haukadalur geothermal area, as it erupts up to 40 m every 4 to 8 minutes, all year long. Strokkur photographs are most often mislabeled as the Geysir.

GPS Coordinates: 64°18′39″ N, 20°18′14″ W

Note: While only one geyser is regularly active, the Haukadalur thermal area features smaller bubbling geysers, steaming fumaroles, colorful and mineral-rich pools, and mud formations. To view live webcam footage of Strokkur's eruptions visit: http://www.livefromiceland.is/webcams/geysir

Cost: Admission and parking to the thermal area is free.

Facilities: Hotel Geyser and the Geysir Glima Restaurant are located directly across the street from the geysers, as is a souvenir shop with restroom facilities. To book a hotel or glance at the menu visit: http://www.geysircenter.is/

Photography: When trying to capture the cresting blue bubble of the Stokkur geyser seconds before the jet erupts 20 m into the air, it is best to keep a watchful eye on the movement of the pooling water. Up to a minute before the eruption, the water will become unruly, and begin sloshing back and forth. You will have less than 5 seconds to capture the fluorescent bubble that forms prior to the eruption. It is best to us a tripod as even the steadiest hands tremble on long exposures, resulting in blurry images. Use burst mode or continuous shooting to capture the eruption in successive motion. Moreover, be vigilant about wiping your lens after each eruption, geyser spray contains silica and calcium carbonate, which results in a hard-to-clean film.

Tip: If the height of the geyser eruption is less than 10m it will more than likely erupt once more in matter of seconds and reach a higher altitude than before. So be on the look out for a double eruption.

ROKKUR

GULLFOSS

Note:
A trail runs from the lower level parking lot along the gorge and to the waterfall. A rock outcrop next to the Gullfoss in between the three steps of the falls provides an amazing up-close view of the powerful water currents and the canyon. Unless your camera is waterproof or is in a waterproof case, be sure to keep your distance from the falls. Be warned that you will get very wet walking to the rock ledge directly by the falls.

Facilities:
A souvenir shop, restaurant, and restroom facilities are located on the upper level parking lot and trail, along with more views of the falls and a distant view of the Langjökull glacier.

GULLFOSS, KNOWN AS THE GOLDEN FALLS for its golden hue on a sunny day, is the post popular attraction in the Golden Circle. The waterfall is located in the canyon of the Hvítá river, whose source is the glacier lake Hvítárvatn at Langjökull glacier. For the first half of the twentieth century, Tómas Tómasson attempted to use the falls to generate electricity, and rented the waterfall to foreign investors. After the many failed attempts due to a lack of funding, electricity was never successfully generated from the waterfall. It is Tómas' daughter, Sigríður Tómasdóttir (whose face is depicted on a stone memorial by the waterfall), who fought vehemently against her fathers desires to utilize the river and the waterfall for industry and profit. It was only after the State of Iceland acquired the property that the waterfall was finally protected.

HEKLA is the second most active volcano in Iceland, and until the 1800's it was thought to be the "gateway to hell" due to its regular and violent eruptions and rumors perpetuated by Cistercian monks. Nevertheless, the actual meaning of the name in Icelandic is a word used to describe a hooded cloak, more or less a reference to the relentless cloud cover over the summit of the volcano. It was only after Icelandic biologist Eggert Ólafsson climbed to the summit in the summer of 1750, that the fear and associations of hell dissipated, and soon there after Hekla became a popular hiking destination. Hekla is a stratovolcano, part of a volcanic ridge in south Iceland, with the most active fissure being the Heklugjá. Due to the large amount of tephra particles Hekla has spewed since its first recorded eruption in 1104, Iceland's

other volcanic eruptions have been dated through the examination of this sediment. The duration of volcanic eruptions along Hekla's ridge is very difficult to predict. Recorded activity has been noted to last as little as a week, to lengthier eruptions lasting as long as a year.

There has been substantial correlation between longer periods of dormancy resulting in greater volcanic eruptions. As of 2010 all signs pointing to a large and imminent eruption have begun taking place, and all travelers are warned to proceed with caution while visiting the mountain.

Do: Visit the multimedia exhibition chronicling the history and the eruptions of the volcano at the Hekla Center at Leirubakki Farm, located 28 km from Mt.Hekla. Admission is five euros, and hours of operation are 10am to 10pm, year round.

Photography: If your ascent up Mt.Hekla is not shrouded by the typically low-lying cloud coverage, you will be rewarded with views of the Fjallabak mountain region of Landmannalaugar, as well as the Vatnajökull glacier

Do: Hike Mt. Hekla by taking either a 2x2 or 4x4 vehicle down route 26, located directly off of the Ring Road. The end of route 26 will lead to the first Hekla marker, and is considered to be the first tier parking lot for 2x2 cars. From this point forward you can continue your journey on foot, which may take as long as 4 hours to reach the summit of the mountain, or you can take your 4x4 to the second tier lot along route F225. From the F225 trailhead, it takes approximately 3 to hours to reach the summit along a relatively straightforward and well-indicated trail. Be forewarned that the descent is long, and the terrain of hardened lava is challenging.

There is also no warden or ranger that oversees this volcanic ridge. Visitors will encounter signage indicating that you are essentially on your own in case of an eruption. For mountain conditions, consult the above-mentioned Hekla Center at Leirubakki Farm. Information is located at http://www.leirubakki.is/

LANDMANNALAUGAR

is a very popular hiking destination in the Fjallabak Nature Reserve in Iceland's southern highlands. Because of its close proximity to Mt.Hekla, the region is a vast expanse of lava fields and multi-colored mountains, which may be seen from the summit of the neighboring volcano. The rhyolite mountains of Landmannalaugar are geologically unusual because they display a variety of colors, the most famous being the Bláhnjúkur and the Brennisteinsalda, with the former translating to "blue peak" and the latter meaning "sulphur wave." Other colors visible in this area include violet, white, turquoise, green, blue, maroon, yellow, and many more.

Unfortunately the weather in the highlands interior tends to be poor, and the beautiful colors of the volcanic desert may appear dull and dark in the persistent rain and low hanging cloud cover. If you happen upon sunshine, you'll be in for a sight. With an abundance of supurb, but often poorly marked hiking trails, anything from a quick two hour hike through the Laugahraun lava field up to the sulphur wave, up to the noted four day Laugavegurinn trail to Þórsmörk is within the realm of possibility.

Note: This part of the highlands is only accessible with a 4x4 vehicle during the high season and the latter part of the shoulder season. Consult with your car hire to verify that driving in the highland interior is covered by your insurance. Due to challenging water currents and deep ford crossings, a vehicle with a high level of clearance and river crossing know-how will serve you greatly in your journey to Landmannalaugar.

Do: Visit the " blue peak" if you are short on time, as it only takes an hour, or visit the Ljótipollur crater lake, also known as the "ugly puddle," if you have four hours to spare. Be sure to check out the steaming sulphur pits just behind the hills of the campsite, and then return to camp to relax from a long day of hiking at the hot spring that runs right through the area.

Shop: The Mountain Mall, a converted green school bus, stocks groceries, toiletries, and other necessities during the high season. The price for such convenience however is not cheap.

SELJALANDSFOSS is an extraordinary waterfall fed by the Seljalandsá river. It was once part of Iceland's former Atlantic Coast line. While its height of sixty meters is not all that impressive compared to many other waterfalls in Iceland, it remains one of the most beautiful. Seljalandsfoss is unique because it has a footpath that goes directly behind the waterfall and exposes the former sea cave, making it possible to see all 360 degrees of its picturesque beauty.

Note: By wearing waterproof clothing you too may go behind the cascading wall of water. Just be sure to wear shoes with sufficient tread. The trail is only wide enough for a single file hike, and through frequent use, much of the path is muddy and wet. Be sure to waterproof your camera equipment as well.

Photography: If the sun is out look for a double rainbow that appears in the mist of the waterfall. If your day is windy look for backwards flowing waterfalls, as the breeze has a tendency to carry the water mist into the sky.

SKÓGAFOSS is another former coastline waterfall fed by the Skógá River, now situated about five kilometers inland since the retreat of the ocean thousands of years ago. The waterfall is a visible border that separates the lower coastal land from the Icelandic Highland terrain just over top of the falls. Legend has it that the 60 meter high fall is the final resting place of the treasure hidden by the first Viking settler Þrasi Þórólfsson before his death. Because of the legend, many locals have attempted to retrieve the treasure from the falls. The story goes to say that one such lucky person managed to affix a rope to the handle of the chest, but the chest broke free while the handle remained on the rope. The handle then became part of the door to the Church of Skógar until 1980, after which it was given to a local museum.

Do: Take the twenty-minute hike up the side of the cliff to the top of the Skógafoss for breathtaking, views towards the Atlantic Ocean. The hike begins as a messy mud path and turns into three flights of stairs. From the top, a step ladder over a fence leads to several additional hiking trails up the Skoga River that reveal many more small waterfalls.

Seljalandsfoss
GPS Coordinates:
63°36'57"N
19°59'34"W
Skógafoss
GPS Coordinates:
63° 31' 47" N
19° 30' 50" W

EYJAFJALLAJÖKULL

The Eyjafjallajökull ice cap covers the caldera of a stratovolcano, whose last eruption on April 14, 2010 caused a slew of flight cancellations and air traffic disruptions, in addition to meltwater floods causing a temporary evacuation of hundreds of Icelanders . The three main peaks of the crater rim, from smallest to largest, are Goðasteinn, Guðnasteinn, and Hámundur, which stands at 1,651 metres. Once part of Iceland's Atlantic coastline several thousand years ago, the ocean has since retreated some five kilometers exposing a steep cliff side, and the well-known Skógafoss. Eyjafjallajökull is part of volcano chain that includes its active subglacial neighbor Katla, just under the Mýrdalsjökull ice cap, with whom the stratavolcano is thought to be geologically related due to a call and response type of activity between them. While the area between the mountain and the coastline is surprisingly flat, the highland roads remain closed until the current and the depths of many fords is deemed passable, following the spring thaw.

Do: Drive inland with a 4x4 to see the base of the Eyjafjallajökull glacier up close. A new lava field from the 2010 eruption will be quite evident. If you are feeling adventurous, book a tour with a reliable mountain guide to summit the new crater. Note that exploring the area on your own via marked gravel roads should only take a couple hours, but a guided hike up the mountain can take up to seven hours.

Do: Stop by the family owned Þorvaldseyri Visitor Centre at the base of the volcano, which opened one year after the start of the April, 2010 Eyjafjallajokull eruption. Watch a short film depicting the events of the eruption and the challenges faced by the family of the Þorvaldseyri farm, as over 3,000 recorded earthquakes shook the region. For more info visit: http://www.icelanderupts.is/

Admission: €5, children under 12 are free.

GPS Coordinates: 63° 32,597'N, 19° 40,043'W to Þorvaldseyri Visitor Centre.

Note:
Even during the high
season, the path to
Eyjafjallajökull consists
of nearly a dozen streams
of various volumes and depths
that need to be forded with a 4x4.
(This photograph features
the third crossing.)

VATNAJÖKULL

National Park

SINCE ITS ESTABLISHMENT in June, 2008, Vatnajökull has become Europe's second largest national park. The park also boasts the islands highest peak, Hvannadalshnjúkur, which has officially been measured to be 2,109.6 meters. In addition to encompassing the Vatnajökull glacier, three additional areas, Lakagígar, Langisjór, and Krepputunga, were added to cover a total 14% of Iceland. This national park is geologically unique because it is home to Europe's largest glacier, Vatnajökull. Beneath the 600m thick ice-cap lie a variety of concealed valleys and subglacial volcanoes, Bárðarbunga being the largest and Grímsvötn erupting most frequently. Vatnajökull's four territories are characterized by a variety of geologically varying landscapes, ranging from a wetland habitat of the wild reindeer and the pink-footed goose, to lush vegetation and mile long ash deposits from the Grímsvötn volcano. Due to the vast expanse of area covered by the park, temperatures vary drastically between the lowlands and the mountains. There is one constant however, which is that nowhere in Iceland does more precipitation fall than in the Vatnajökull area. Due to persistent and violent subglacial floods known as jökulhlaup, the low area is scarcely used for farming, even though the land is more fertile here than anywhere else on the island.

GPS Coordinates: 64°01′00.1″N, 16° 57′57.8″W

Note: Parks formerly known as Skaftafell and Jökulsárgljúfur were absorbed under the Vatnajökull National Park name. There are also very few gas stations in the area, so be sure to head out to the park with a sufficient amount of petrol. Moreover, unlike much of the island, there are no roads leading into the interior of the National Park.

Facilities: Skaftafell Visitors Centre is open year around to provide information about weather, activities, trails, and trail conditions. Hours of operation vary from season to season, so be sure to obtain up-to-date information at: http://www.vatnajokulsthjodgardur.is/english/

Admission: Entrance to the park is free. Restrooms and parking are on premise and free to use as well.

Do: This is one of the seldom times that I will recommend hiring a third party for an activity, but it is certainly one not to be missed, and should not be attempted alone. Book a glacier hike from any of the companies listed in the book, and head out on a 2, 4, or even 6-hour adventure on the magnificent blue ice.

JÖKULSÁRLÓN

Glacial River Lagoon

JÖKULSÁRLÓN literally means "glacial river lagoon," and its location along the Ring Road at the edge of Vatnajökull National Park makes it a frequently visited destination. Before the lake first developed some 68 years ago, the Breiðamerkurjökull glacier once sat right along the Atlantic shoreline, depositing icebergs into the ocean. As it receded further into the land, the glacier left behind deep gorges. These gorges now form the glacial river Jökulsárlón, which continues to grow at rate dependent on the melting of the glacier, increasing fourfold since the 1970's. Fed by the melt water and ice from neighboring glaciers, icebergs gather at mouth of the lakes exit until they are small enough to pass on into the sea. Iceland's natural wonder has since become a highlight in many movies, shows, and music videos, as the owners of the lake frequently lease it out for filming and commercial use.

GPS Coordinates: 64° 4′ 13″ N, 16° 12′ 42″ W

Do: Walk along the black sand shoreline and note the two shades of color in which the icebergs form. Depending on the amount of air trapped within the ice, light crystals can appear a brilliant blue or a milky white. Be on the lookout for varying iceberg forms shaped by ancient ash deposits from eruptions long ago. If you feel a pressing need to venture into the ice cold water, do so with the aid of an amphibious vehicle available through a commercial boat excursion company at the banks of the lagoon. Since the first commercial boat company began its operation in 1985, some 900,000 tourists have taken a tour of the lagoon.

Photography: Jökulsárlón is a nesting area for a great variety of sea birds; the black sand deposits in particular make up the main habitat of the Skua. With an overabundance of krill and fish, one can always spot Arctic Terns, Gannets, and even a colony of seals.

VÍK Í MÝRDAL

The costal village of Vík may be small, but there is a great deal of sights to see; because of its location along the Ring Road, doing so is quite easy. This village may have less than three hundred inhabitants, but it is the most populated settlement for miles around, thus it is an important hub for food and refueling. The church upon the hill in Vík plays an important role to the inhabitants of this town, as it is thought to be the only place that could survive the glacial flood brought on by Katla's future eruption.

See: Vík's black sand beach has been named one of the most beautiful beaches around the world, and if you can catch the sun rising through the black needle columns know as Reynisdrangar, and you'll see why.

Bird Watching: A wide array of seabirds, including puffins, may be seen encircling the coastline during the nesting season.

Photography: If you can make it to the beach before dusk you will catch an enthralling contrast of sunset colors against the stark black sand and grey basalt columns.

L

LAKAGÍGAR IS A fissure part of the volcanic system of the Grímsvötn and Þórðarhyrna volcanoes that lie between the Mýrdalsjökull and Vatnajökull glaciers. The June 1783 fissure eruption lasted until February 1784, and spewed such a high volume of hydrofluoric acid and sulfuric aerosols, that nearly half of Iceland's livestock was decimated. This event, in turn, caused a famine that lead to the starvation of a quarter of Iceland's human population, and is thought to be responsible for many more lives lost in Europe following the aftermath.

HALLORMSTAÐUR

Is the largest forested area in Iceland. The area has been under protection, by law, for over 100 years, and reforestation efforts have yet to slow since their largest undertaking in 1950. To date, the forest covers an 18km long stretch around the glacial lake, Logurinn. The River Lagarfljót, made famous through the legend of its resident, the Lagarfljót Worm Monster, flows through Lake Logurinn in the Hallormstaður forest. The forest features an outdoor art exhibit, and a variety of events, including the Icelandic lumberjacking championship. For more information visit www.hallormsstadur.is

SEYÐISFJÖRÐUR

Is not exactly a sight, but rather a sight to behold. This picturesque town in the east fjords of Iceland, sits serenely in a valley surrounded by mountains some 27km from Egilsstaðir. The climax of a journey to Seyðisfjörður is none other than the Fjarðarheiði Mountain road that connects the small town to the remainder of Iceland. An other worldly sight of snow-capped mountain peaks and endless blue skies give way to reveal a cascading waterfall and a postcard-like settlement at the bottom of a lush green fjord. With Mt.Bjólfur to the west and Mt.Strandartindur to the east, even the midnight sun is no match for the shadow that creeps over the colorful wooden houses at dusk. The town even has its own website: www.visitseydisfjordur.com/

GPS Coordinates: 65°15′37″ N, 14°0′14″ W

DETTIFOSS

The 100 meter wide waterfall, descending 45 meters down the Jökulsárgljúfur canyon, is part of the protected Vatnajökull National Park territory in northeast Iceland. Views of the waterfall may be had from both the east and the west bank of the Jökulsá á Fjöllum river, However, the sheer spray on the west side makes it less desirable for photography. In terms of volume discharge, Dettifoss is the largest waterfall in Europe, making it one of the most popular tourist destinations within the Diamond Circle. Unlike the Gullfoss waterfall in the Golden Circle, which appears brown, the water gushing down Dettifoss is rich with glacial melt water sediments that give it a milky appearance.

GPS Coordinates: 65°49'18.91" N, 16°23'17.41" W

NOTE

Due to the fact that the river is only bridged in one particular section of the Ring Road, you will have to choose on which side you wish to proceed with during your visit. Whether or not time is a factor, the east bank is the better advised, particularly for 2x2 cars.

East Bank: In addition to an information panel, restroom facilities, parking, and an all around better approach road, the east bank boasts a narrow footpath down to the waterfall for some of the best points of view.

West Bank: The grassy slope on the west bank is a rather muddy mess, due to constant water spray from west prevailing winds. Neither bank features a guardrail, so be sure to proceed with caution.

HVERIR

HVERARÖNDOR HVERIR:

Along your drive on the Ring Road, your sense of smell will be accosted by what can only be described as a sack of eggs festering in the desert sun. By all appearances it will also seem as though you have stumbled upon a god-forsaken desert where nothing could survive. Nevertheless, the fauna rich oasis of the Mývatn Nature Reserve is only a stones throw away. Welcome to the other-worldly Namafjall area, destination Hveraröndor hot springs, a place where no vegetation can be sustained. This colorfully sulphurous landscape is nestled in the foothills of a volcano and surrounded by chain of snow-capped mountains. Nothing in Iceland compares to the bubbling mud pots, called solfataras, and the steam springs known as fumaroles. Depending on the day, the weather, and the season, it is possible to see entirely different colors in the landscape than anyone before you.

GPS Coordinates:
65°38'32.46" N,
16°48'26.82" W

Note: Nothing can prepare you for the nauseating emission of sulphuric fumes the will envelope you the moment a gust of wind blows them in your direction. It is a smell that you almost cannot get used to. My advice is to wear sunglasses, as the light-colored earth is extremely reflective. If you will be lingering longer than most people in order to take photos, grab an extra shirt or a shawl to wrap around your face. A spot of water or a wet wipe tucked into the section of the item you are wrapping around your face will make a world of a difference for your breathing comfort.

Tip for a 4x4: When you exit the Hveraröndor Hverir parking lot heading towards Mývatn, there will be a hidden unmarked turn off to your left. If you blink, you will miss it! It is located immediately following your last glance of the mud springs. Follow this road to a small dirt pull-off, where there is sufficient parking for several cars. You will be rewarded with panoramic views from the top of the hill overlooking the colorful landscape of Hverir, in addition to interesting formations located on top of the hill that cannot be seen from below.

BJARNARFLAG GEOTHERMAL POWER PLANT: On the route to Mývatn lake you will encounter a man made lake of such luminous blue brilliance that it appears almost radioactive to the touch. While the water is safe, it does contain a different mineral composition and elevated silica levels, such as the pools of the Blue Lagoon. This small lake is property of the Bjarnarflag **geothermal power plant** that sits on the banks with a single, steam-emitting pipe. There are plans to develop the small Bjarnarflag into a larger capacity power plant, despite raised concerns over aquatic and aviary ecosystem disruption in the Mývatn region.

GPS Coordinates: 65° 38' 22.28" N ,
16° 50' 59.04" W

Mývatn Lake: Created some 2300 years ago by a fissure eruption, this shallow and nutrient rich lake is named after the large number of Midges that inhabit the area. Due to the high content of nutrients fed into the lake via spring water, the lake produces enough algae and **crustaceans** to sustain the thirteen species of migratory ducks that nest in the area. Several more species of duck may be found in the neighboring river Laxa, into which Mývatn drains, making this protected water system a very important part of the water-fowl habitat. For a guide of birds in Mývatn and the northeast Iceland, consult: www.birdingtrail.is/

GPS Coordinates: 65°36′0″ N, 17°0′0″ W

LEIRHNJÚKUR:

Just west of the geothermal power station is an alien-like landscape known as the Leirhnjúkur lava field. Part of the same volcanic system as Krafla, this site is a visible remnant of the "Krafla Fires." Take time to explore well-marked trails, as they reveal boiling hot pots and an array of textured and colored soil. Older, moss-covered lava from eighteenth century eruptions will give way to darker, newer formations from the last forty decades. Be cautious around soil with markings of white and yellow as they indicate under ground steam vents, of which your nose will quickly notify you, as the air will smell of rotting eggs in such places.

KRAFLA:

Is a well known caldera in the Mývatn region. This geological formation is usually formed when a magma chamber builds up, and then collapses under intense volcanic pressure. Krafla first gained notoriety during the 70's and 80's when frequent eruptions of lava were dubbed the "Krafla Fires." Due to favorably shallow lying magma in this region, Krafla has been the site of a geothermal power station since 1977, and the present day site of a well developed by the Iceland Deep Drilling Project.

KRÖFLUSTÖÐ:
If you are interested in learning
about the process of converting
geothermal heat into electricity visit
Kröflustöð, Krafla's geothermal power station.
The plant offers a free exhibit Monday-Friday
12:30 to 3:30pm and 1 to 5pm on the weekends.
For further information about
the plant visit www.landsvirkjun.com/

GPS Coordinates: 65° 35′ 25″ N,
16° 53′ 58″ W

Facilities:
The Leirhnjúkur area has free parking and
restrooms on premises, just past the power station.

Do: If time permits, and you have around eight hours to spare,
consider hiking a trail known as the Krafla Route. The trail will take
you from the Leirhnjúkur lava field to the small village Reykjahlíð, all
while crossing over lava that first erupted in the seventeen hundreds.
Give yourself 3 to 4 hours for the trip there, and another few for the trip back.

See: Askja's Víti Crater contains a stunningly opaque crater lake, a quick five-
minute drive from the Leirhnjúkur lava fields. While several people have
swam in the comfortably warm waters, it is always a good idea to proceed
with caution as carbon dioxide has a tendency to gather at the surface of
the water, causing bathers to pass out and potentially drown. While
traveling the circumference of this once hellish crater, take heed
of the gusty breeze, and enjoy the beautiful turquoise
tranquility of this mineral-rich lake.

GPS Coordinates: 65°43′4.02″ N,
16°45′8.14″ W

DIMMUBORGIR

There is a great deal of things to see in the Mývatn area, including the "dark castles" known as Dimmuborgir. The name comes from the lava field's unusually tall and looming structural shapes, which stand up to ten meters tall. Of all of the Dimmuborgir rock formations, the most famous is the one that resembles the ruins of an ancient citadel. Nevertheless, it is nothing more than a collapsed lava tube formed through contact between lava and water, 2,300 years ago. There are many volcanic caves and hollow lava pillars to explore in the area, thus they are aptly know as in Norwegian lore as "The Catacombs of Hell."

GPS Coordinates: 65°35'27.94" N, 16°54'37.15" W

ASKJA

Located in the remote Icelandic highlands, and surrounded by the Dyngjufjöll mountains, Askja, a stratovolcano, is only accessible by car during the high season. Askja lay dormant and undiscovered until violent eruptions in the spring of 1875 lead to heavy ashfalls that killed livestock, and prompted a rush of emigration to safer parts of the island. Askja's last recorded eruption occurred in 1961. There has been much concern as of late, however, due to seismic activity and an increase of geothermal activity in the caldera's lake.

GPS Coordinates: 65°1'48"N, 16°45'0" W

Do: If you have a day to spare between late June and mid September, take route F88 just east of the Mývatn down to F894. Or you can hire a third party company in the area of the Mývatn Nature Reserve for a day trip to the crater. Once at Askja you'll be able to see the very place that the Appolo program has used in the past to prepare for lunar assignments.

Note: If you can't spare the time, no worries, Víti's crater lake in the northeast is nearly identical to the larger Askja.

Tip:
Keep your glasses on and your mouth closed during the hike, much of the loose sand will pelt you in the face as you ascend to the top. The winds are much stronger closer to the rim.

HVERFJALL

It takes approximately half an hour to climb up the steep, sliding sediment tephra cone to see the crater of the Hverfjall volcano. The tephra that forms the entire shape of this mountain has been scattered all over the Myvatn area since it last erupted in 2500 BP. What can you expect to see inside the 1 km long diameter of the crater you may wonder? Absolutely nothing. This will either make or break your decision to set course along the strenuous, uphill hike. The top of the crater has a thin two-foot wide path encircling the rim, and the interior of the crater is full of more of the same black tephra. The view from the top is serene, and the landscape is foreign and moon-like. If you have time and energy to spare, go for it.

HVERFJALL

AKUREYRI

Is the second largest populated town after the capital city of Reykjavík. As such, it has acquired the name "The Capital of the North." Akureyri's harbor has been the key role in growing the city from a dozen settling merchants and fishermen, to a sizable city of nearly twenty thousand. The area's geographical location also play's a hand in the city's fast growing expansion, as the area experiences a relatively mild and steady climate. Nevertheless, with an average of only 43 sunny days annually, you certainly won't need to wear your sunglass in this cloudy town.

GPS Coordinates: 65°41′0″ N, 18°6′0″ W

Do: Take some time off from driving and grab one of the many whale-watching or sea-angling tours available from Akureyri's harbor.

GLYMUR

If have time to spare on your return journey to Reykjavík, and want to skip the long tunnel, you will be rewarded with views of the Glymur waterfall on the surface route. Located in the Hvalfjörður area, this is Iceland's second tallest waterfall, at 196 meters in height. Since the opening of the tunnel under the Hvalfjörður fjord in 1998, many travelers have missed the beautiful sights of this area in an effort to reduce their travel times. There are several trails leading to viewpoints of the falls from the Botnsá parking area, the north trail being the easiest.

GPS Coordinates: 64°23′45″ N, 21°14′28″ W

**<u>Are the Glacier hikes
for everyone?</u>**
Not all excursions are
suited for everyone, however
the options provided by most
companies have a wide enough
range of accessibility
to people of varying
fitness abilities.

GLACIER HIKING

With an abundance of experienced and reliable guides to choose from, it has never been easier for people from all walks of life and fitness levels to partake in the once-in-a-lifetime experience of glacier walking. A majority of guide-led glacier excursions are available May through September, and must be booked with third party providers well in advance during the high season.

Frequently Asked Questions

Can I bring my camera on a Glacier hike?
Absolutely, in fact the views are positively majestic on a sunny day.

Can I wear jeans on the hike?
Jeans are not recommended for several reasons, primarily being that they limit your mobility and do not provide adequate heat isolation. Most importantly however, jeans are not fast drying, and whether you are walking or hiking on a glacier, you may never know for sure if your footing will give way to a stream or a crevice.

Do I have to book the hike in advance?
Yes, it is highly encouraged to book a glacier hike at least three weeks in advance, especially if your travel time falls between mid-June to late-August. If you are traveling during shoulder season, booking in advance ensures that the scheduled departure times will not be cancelled if the minimum amount of participants have not signed up.

Do I need to bring a lunch and/or a backpack?
If your hike exceeds 2.5 hours, it is advisable to bring a snack or a lunch in a backpack. Moreover, with an abundance of fresh ice melt, you can also pack several empty water bottles, and fill them up with true Icelandic Glacial water.

What is the difference between 2.5 hikes and 4 to 5 hour hikes?
The main difference between these trips is that shorter hikes vary by location from the longer hikes. Shorter hikes are geared towards those with a lower range of physical fitness, or persons short on time. Hikers on shorter trips, such as the 2.5 hour hikes, tend to spend approximately one hour on the ice after the short drive to the tongue of the glacier, and the safety briefing. Short trips explore the lower retreat of a glacier that consists of gradual inclines and no ice-axe climbing. These trips are slow in pace, and offer splendid views of the glacier mountainsides, which is perfect for picture taking. If you are able to walk a mile, and have little to no hip or knee issues, you should have no difficulties partaking in a 2.5-hour hike. With four to five hour trips, you should subtract one hour to accommodate for the drive and the safety briefing. Longer trips explore the glacier more thoroughly, and hikers get to put their ice-axes to use for both stability and vertical climbing. These types of hikes require a higher level of agility and fitness. If you are able to walk three miles with varying terrain and inclines, you should be able to partake in a longer hike.

Can you see the "Crystal Cave" in the summer?
Unfortunately, due to the delicate nature of ice caves, it is unlikely you will be able to gain entrance to them during the summer months. Cold temperatures help regulate the volume and size of glacier rivers that otherwise run at full flow during the high season, making it unsafe to enter caves.

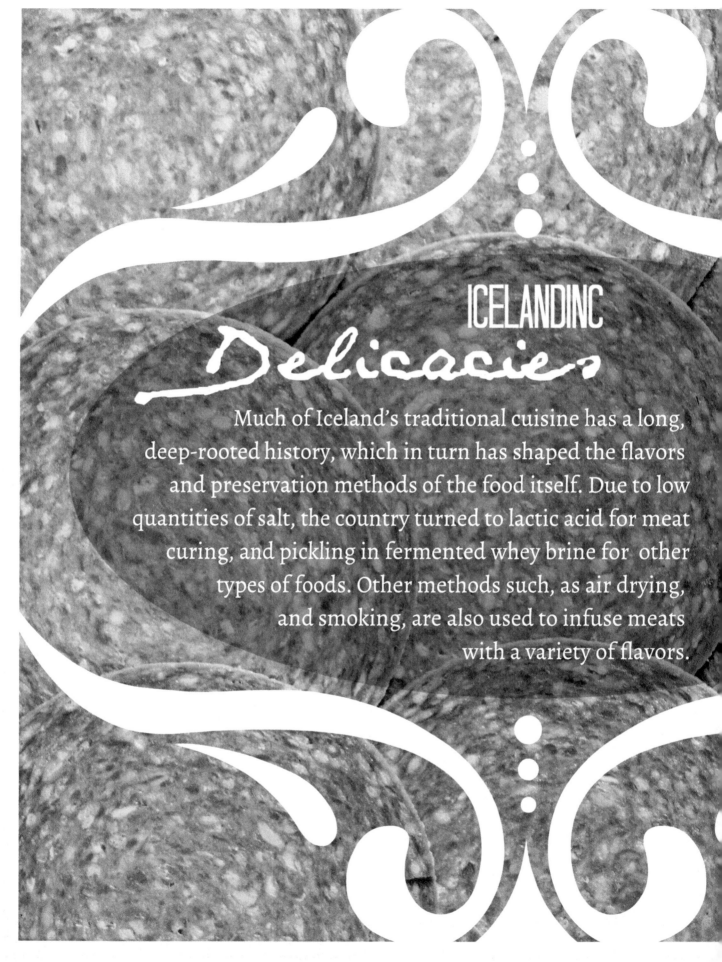

ICELANDINC
Delicacies

Much of Iceland's traditional cuisine has a long, deep-rooted history, which in turn has shaped the flavors and preservation methods of the food itself. Due to low quantities of salt, the country turned to lactic acid for meat curing, and pickling in fermented whey brine for other types of foods. Other methods such, as air drying, and smoking, are also used to infuse meats with a variety of flavors.

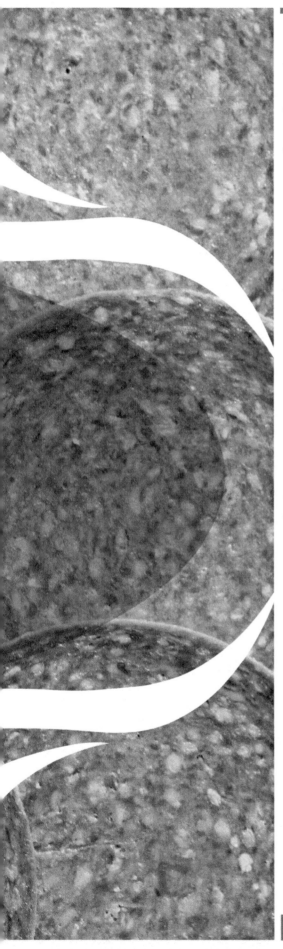

Brennivín: Clear, unsweetened schnapps

Fiskibollur: Ground fish and potatoes formed into a ball

Gellur: The muscle beneath a Cod's tongue

Hákarl: Fermented shark meat

Hangikjöt: Smoked and boiled lamb, mutton, or horse meat

Harðfiskur: Dried fish eaten with dollop of butter

Hrútspungar: Lambs testicles soured in whey

Hvalspik: Whale fat cured in lactic acid

Kútmagar: Stuffed and boiled fish stomach

Lifrarpylsa: Liver sausage

Mjólkursoðinn lundi: Boiled Puffin in milk sauce

Þorramatur: Traditional buffet of cured meats and fish products served at midwinter festivals

Rúgbrauð: Sweet and dense dark rye bread

Selshreifar: Seal meat cured in lactic acid

Skyr: Cultured dairy product, which comes in many flavors and tastes similar to Greek yogurt

Slátur: Blood pudding made from sheep innards

Súr Hvalur: Sour whale meat

Svið: Singed and boiled sheep's head

RESTAURANTS
Eat, Drink and be Merry

Bernhöftsbakarí

Dining options: Breakfast/Brunch €
Cuisines: Bakery, Café
Address: Bergstaðarstræti 13, 101 Reykjavík
Hours: Weekdays: 7:30am - 6pm, Weekends: 8am - 5pm

Popular with the locals, this bakery is known for baking breads on hot stone since 1834. Stop by and enjoy a variety of fairly priced chocolate scones, handmade breads, and custard filled doughnuts with your morning coffee.

Bakarí Sandholt

Dining options: Breakfast/Brunch €€
Cuisines: Bakery, French, Café, and Sandwiches
Address: Laugavegur 36, Reykjavík
Hours: Monday-Thursday 6:30am - 7pm, Friday-Sunday 6:30am - 9pm

Open earlier than most breakfast places around town, this little bakery is more than just a walk-up counter at the end of a main shopping street. Enjoy a wide array of fresh baked breakfast pastries, coffee, a soup of the day, and delicious sandwiches you can take on your Icelandic adventures.

Laundromat Café

Dining options: Breakfast/Brunch €€€
Cuisines: Variety
Address: Austurstræti 9, Reykjavík
Hours: Monday-Wednesday 8am – 12am, Thursday-Friday 8am – 1am, Saturday 10am- 1am, Sunday 10am – 12am

This little gem can be tough to get into, which is the only downside of a fortunately delicious menu that leaves you drooling as you wait for a table while locals chow down on gigantic portions. Once you are seated, you may pass the time between your order and the arrival of your meal with free Wi-Fi.

Nudluskalin

Dining options: Lunch/Dinner €
Cuisines: Noodle Shop
Address: Skolavordustig 8, Reykjavík
Hours: Monday-Friday 11:30am - 9pm, Saturday 12pm - 8pm

Nudluskalin is a great option for great food on a budget. While the interior décor leaves a bit to be desired, the food is delicious, quick, and fairly priced, especially for Iceland. Noodle bowls contain a variety of fresh ingredients, and the soups are great on a cold and rainy Icelandic day.

Kruska Reykjavík

Dining options: Lunch/Dinner €€
Cuisines: Vegetarian, Healthy
Address: Sudurlandsbraut 12, Reykjavík
Hours: Weekdays 11am - 9pm

Experience a variety of wholesome and fresh prepared food, such as vegetable lasagna, Moroccan stew, and even Piri Piri Chicken. While the menu is known for a wide array of vegetarian dishes, the most notable dish at Kruska is the popular "chicken of the day."

Gallery Fiskur

Dining options: Lunch €€€
Cuisines: Dessert, Seafood
Address: Nethylur 2, Reykjavík
Hours: Monday – Friday 11:30am - 2pm

Open only on weekdays from 11:30 am to 2:00pm, this seafood restaurant boasts a variety of local Icelandic fish in a dining area decorated with art created by local Icelandic artists. If you have access to a working kitchen, stop by the Gallerý Fiskur fish shop, conveniently located next door, and pick up fresh fish from large selection of high quality and local products.

A Guide to Dining in Iceland

Gló
Dining Options: Lunch/Dinner €
Cuisines: Healthy, Vegetarian
Address: Laugavegur 20b, Reykjavík
Hours: Weekends and Weekdays 11 am – 9 pm,
The concept of Gló is fresh, healthy food, with a wide array of selections. The cafeteria-style line lets you select a main entrée with an accompaniment of three different sides. Non-vegetarian options are available as well.

Kopar
Dining options: Dinner €€
Cuisines: Contemporary
Address: Geirsgata 3, Reykjavík
Hours: Monday - Thursday 11:30am - 10:30pm, Friday 11:30am -11:30pm, Saturday 12:00pm -11:30pm, Sunday 6pm - 10:30pm
Kopar is Icelandic fare with a modern twist and local ingredients, in a trendy atmosphere. As with all Icelandic restaurants you can be certain that the "catch of the day" is as fresh as it gets. If you're in the mood for a sweet but not too sweet cocktail, give the Honey Lemon Vodka a try, it's divine. Want a window view? Book a table online at www.koparrestaurant.is

Kol
Dining Options: Weekday Lunch/Dinner anytime €€€
Cuisines: Delicatessen, International, and Grill
Address: Skólavörðustígur 40 in Reykjavík
Hours: Monday-Friday11.30am -11pm, Saturday-Sunday 5.30pm – 11pm
The new hot spot in town is Kol, so come prepared with reservations, and be ready to enjoy classic Icelandic comfort food with a new twist. The atmosphere is an open kitchen and a trendy bar with a variety of tablescapes and cozy leather couches. For reservations: http://kolrestaurant.is/

Lebowski Bar
Dining Options: Lunch/Dinner €
Cuisines: American Pub
Address: Laugarvegur 20a, Reykjavík
Hours: Sunday-Thursday 11:30pm – 1am, Friday-Saturday 11:30pm – 4am
Fairly priced American pub food, with generous portions, a relaxed atmosphere, and a good bar with Guinness. Whether or not you are a lover of this Coen Brothers' classic, the movie-influenced décor might win you over.

Svarta Kaffið
Dining Options: Lunch/Dinner €€
Cuisines: Soup
Address: Laugavegi 54, Reykjavík
Hours: Sunday-Thursday 11am - 1am, Friday-Saturday 11am – 3 am
The rich homemade soups served in a rustic bread bowl at Svarta Kaffið are enough to quell anyone's desires for warm and filling comfort food. Each day of the week brings two new "soups of the day" to the menu, typically one vegetable, and the other meat. The cozy wooden atmosphere, and fair selection of craft beer is not too shabby either.

Restaurants in Hveragerði
Hverabakarí Sf
Dining Options: Breakfast/Brunch €
Cuisines: Bakery, Café
Address: Breidumork 10, Hveragerði
Hours: Monday-Friday 8:30am – 6pm, Saturday-Sunday 9am – 6pm
Located on the main street of Hveragerði, this bakery is famous for its traditional hot spring bread. In addition to an array of baked goods and an abundance of seating, the bakery also offers dairy products, cakes, and hot dogs.

Restaurants in Hveragerði

HOFLANDSSETRIÐ
Dining Options: Bar/Dinner €€
Cuisines: Pizza, Burger, and Specials
Address: Breidumork, Hveragerði
Hours: Monday-Sunday 11:30am – 10pm
A large menu featuring a wide array of options, from made to order pizzas and burgers, to a trout and lamb chop special. This is a popular place to watch sports and take it easy after a long day of driving.

Restaurant Varmá
Dining Options: Bar/Dinner €€€
Cuisines: Icelandic
Address: Hverhamar, Hveragerði
Hours: Sunday-Thursday 7pm – 9pm, Friday-Saturday 7pm – 10pm
From brown bread baked in the neighboring geothermal hot pots, to the "Taste of Iceland" appetizer platter, restaurant Varmá exudes tradition and authenticity mixed with a touch of modern flare.
 Make reservations at www.frostogfuni.is/restaurant-varma/about/

Kjöt og Kúnst
Dining Options: Café/Lunch/Dinner €€
Cuisines: Icelandic
Address: Breioumork 21, Hveragerði
Hours: Monday-Saturday 12pm – 9mp
The special lunch menu features a "dish of the day" everyday, in addition to a buffet of soups and fresh baked bread. The summer months usher in a variety of dinner buffets, as well as a grill and an À la carte menu that is available year around. Here, you may also sample a variety of Icelandic staples such as fried fish balls, and air dried fish with butter.

Restaurants in Höfn

Hafnarbúðin
Dining Options: Brunch/Lunch/Dinner €
Cuisines: Icelandic
Address: Ránarslóð 2, Höfn
Hours: High Season: 8am – 11pm, Off Season 9am – 11:30pm
This little, yellow harbor store/diner is home to the best hot dogs on the island (get them with everything). Come here for cheap, and reliable comfort food. A haven if you're coming in late from a daylong adventure, and nothing but a lobster hoagie or fish and chips will do.

Kaffi Hornið
Dining Options: Dinner €€
Cuisines: International
Address: Hafnarbraut 42, Höfn
Hours: High Season 10am - 11:30pm, Shoulder Season 10am - 10pm, Off Season 10am - 1pm
If you're in the mood for a Langoustine platter, but don't feel like dressing the part, rejoice in the cozy, wooden cabin atmosphere of the Kaffi Hornið. Vegetarians have something to celebrate here too, it's the well know pan-fried chickpea cutlets. While the crustacean soup is a bit of a specialty, the wild reindeer burgers don't disappoint either.

Pakkhús
Dining Options: Café/Dinner/Bar €€€
Cuisines: International
Address: Krosseyjarvegi 3, Höfn
Pakkhús sits overlooking the harbor in Höfn í Hornafjörður, a place so well know for its Langoustines that the town throws a festival to celebrate them. It goes with out saying that there is an abundance of versatile Langoustine dishes on the restaurants menu, so be prepared to de-shell the saucy and buttery crustaceans yourself.

Restaurants in Seyðisfjörður

Hotel Aldan Restaurant

Dining Options: Breakfast, Lunch and Dinner €€€
Cuisines: European
Address: Nordurgata 2, Seyðisfjörður
This charming, old, historical house by the harbor, features a traditional Icelandic menu, made up of local materials specific to the season. During the high season, the Aldan is open for breakfast, lunch and dinner. Cakes, light meals, and Italian coffee are sold at the café.

Bistro Skaftfell

Dining Options: Late Night €€
Cuisines: European
Address: Austurvegur 42, Seyðisfjörður
Hours: Everyday 12pm - 9:30pm
Furnished in the spirit of artists everywhere, this eclectic and eccentric bistro is well-known for their reindeer pizza, a good vibe, and a sweet slice of cake. Be sure to check out their eccentric and ever changing art display in the gallery upstairs at the conclusion of your meal. Wi-fi is available for patrons of the restaurant.

Kaffi Lara - El Grillo Bar

Dining Options: Bar, Café €€
Cuisines: International
Address: Nordurgata 3, Seyðisfjörður
Hours: Monday-Thursday 11:30 – 1:30am,
Friday-Saturday 11:30 – 3:30am,
Sunday 12:30pm – 1:30am
Kaffi Lara features a variety of handmade cakes and pastries, and house made beer who's lables feature the face of the original owner. Brunch is served every Sunday between the hours of 1pm-4pm, and BBQ is on the menu every Wednesday and Saturday from 5pm-8pm. Ask about the local legend, Lara.

Restaurants in Mývatn

Vogafjos Cowshed Café

Dining options: Breakfast, Lunch and Dinner €€€
Cuisines: Icelandic
Address: Vogafjosi 660, Mývatn
Hours: 7:30am – 11pm
Surprisingly located in a dairy barn, this little café serves up a variety of homemade cheeses and ice cream, in addition to a variety of local and seasonal Icelandic dishes. Look for signature dishes prepared with Artic char, smoked trout, and raw smoked lamb, served alongside geothermally-baked bread. After dinner you can stop by the cowshed and observe cows being milked and fed.

Daddi`s Pizza

Dining options: Lunch and Dinner €
Cuisines: Pizza
Address: Vogar, Mývatn
Hours: 11:30am – 11pm
Signature pizzas prepared using local ingredients as toppings. Try the famed rosted pine nut and smoked trout (fresh from Mývatn Lake) combination, of which Icelanders as far as Reykjavík rave about. With each pizza named after a sight in Iceland, you no longer have to be content with just looking at sights, Daddi`s pizza lets you taste them as well.

Kaffi Borgir

Dining Options: Café €€
Cusines: Icelandic
Address: Dimmuborgir, Mývatn
Hours: April: 11am-2pm, May: 10am-4pm, June-August: 9am-10pm, September: 10am-5pm
Located in one of the most scenic spots in the Myvatn area, Kaffi Borgir overlooks the lake, and the Dimmuborgir formations. The Café offers a selection of local specialties, light meals, such as pre-made sandwiches and soups, and A La Carte dinner menu.

Kristjan's Bakari & Café
Dining Options: Café, Dessert €
Cuisines: Bakery
Address: Hafnarstraeti 108, Akureyri
Kristjan's offers a wide range of breakfast pastries, such as scones, croissants, and pre-made sandwiches, along with other handmade creations. Coffee and tea are available to help you start the day. It is reasonably priced (by Icelandic standards), and since we stopped by on a weekday morning, we were the only customers at that hour. The service is friendly, and the bottomless coffee goes best with an Icelandic doughnut, which are lighter in consistency and texture than a standard American doughnut.

Blaa Kannan Café
Dining options: Breakfast/Brunch, Late Night €€
Cuisines: Café, Variety
Address: Hafnarstraeti 96, Akureyri
This charming café on Akureyri's main shopping street doesn't feature a plethora of menu items, but still manages to entice you with its cozy wooden interior, free coffee refills, daily baked quiches, and panini sandwiches. Great if you are not looking for a large, sit-down meal.

Kaffi Ilmur
Dining options: Breakfast/Brunch $$
Cuisines: Coffee Shop, Dessert, Icelandic
Address: Hafnarstraeti 107 b, Akureyri
This little, yellow house on a hill is a welcoming sight to sore pockets. For 1990 ISK you may have a go at Ilmur's lunch buffet, with a choice of homemade soup, fresh baked bread, an all you can eat salad bar, and two different meat dishes. Of course the ever changing selection of desserts and hot coffee are just as easy on your wallet.

Örkin hans Nóa
Dining options: Reservations, Late Night € € €
Cuisines: Seafood
Address: Hafnarstraeti 22, Akureyri 600
Hours: Everyday from 6pm - 10pm
Noa provides an eccentric and cozy atmosphere, with attentive service and a chef who is accommodating and innovative with requests for vegetarian entrees. Most of the food arrives panfried, in individual and generous skillets that are brought to your table for sharing, or indulging on your own.

Hamborgarafabrikkan
Dining Options: Lunch, Dinner € €
Cuisines: American, Barbecue, Hamburgers, International
Address: Hafnarstraeti 87-89 | Hotel KEA, Akureyri 600
Hours: Sunday-Thursday 11pm - 10pm, Friday-Saturday 11pm - 12am
The Hamburger Factory is a huge hit in Akureyri for those who have tired of lamb and seafood. With a menu comprised of 16 types of burgers (including the winning "Best Veggie Burger of 2011"), ribs, wings, and salads, it is sure to satisfy those cravings for comfort food.

Bryggjan
Dining options: Lunch, Dinner € €
Cuisines: Bistro, Gastropub, Family Fare
Address: Strandgata 49 | 600 Akureyri
Hours: Sunday-Thursday 11:30am - 9:30pm, Friday-Saturday 12:30pm - 10pm.
Fairly priced pizza, with good portion sizes and friendly service. In addition to pizza, the resteraunt offers a wide variety of pub fare and Icelandic beer.

AUGUST

Verslunarmannahelgi
Aug 1-4th

A celebration of some type is sure to be found anywhere you go in Iceland during this labor/bank holiday weekend. A wide array of barbecues, music, and sports will be sure to provide a good time for families, partiers, and passersby, while towns honor Icelandic merchants with a day off. This is usually the biggest weekend for domestic travel for Icelanders, and many leave the city behind for camping trips and National Parks.

Reykjavík Gay Pride
Aug 5-10th

Reykjavik Pride is a nearly weeklong event, attracting several thousand international visitors to its whimsical and colorful set of events. The 2014 commemorated the sixteenth pride event in the city of Reykjavik, and has undoubtedly become one of the most sought out events in Reykjavík's cultural event's calendar. Pride Passes are sold at the Reykjavík Pride Center at Lækjargata 2a. More info on this event and the parade route can be found at www.reykjavikpride.com or by visiting Reykjavík Pride on Facebook.

Þjóðhátíð
First week of August

Is an annual outdoor festival part of the Verslunarmannahelgi holiday, held in Vestmannaeyjar Iceland. Each year thousands of locals and visitors flock to Heimaey island, which only has the capacity for about 4200, for four days of various live music. In 2010 nearly 17,000 were in attendance to enjoy the big stage concerts, a kick-off bonfire, mid-event fireworks shows, and signature Sunday night crowd singing finale. Þjóðhátíð began in 1874 when Westman islanders were unable to celebrate the one-thousand-year anniversary of Icelandic settlement on the mainland, due to bad weather and sailing conditions. Since then the festival has become the largest of its kind, and may one day far exceed the capacity of the Westman Islands. With a limited number of proper accommodations many people set up camp right in the middle of all of the action. It is important to arrive well rested, as sleep might only be available occasionally if you are attending for all four days. To purchase tickets or view the program visit: http://www.dalurinn.is/en

The Great Fish Day
Aug 8-10th
The Great Fish day is an annual festival in Dalvíkurbyggð, 45 km north of Akureyri. Locals and visitors alike are all welcome dine for free on what seems like a never-ending sea food buffet between the hours of 11:00am and 5pm at the harbor in Dalvík. This generous festival was created to get as many people as possible to taste fresh and local Icelandic fish. There is a wide variety of other menu items available in addition to traditional Icelandic ones. With an assembly line of grills, marinades, and beverages, this event is sure to satisfy everyone's tastes.

Reykjavík Jazz Festival
August 14-20th
This four day long event has been making international headlines in the world of Jazz. Enjoy a popular showcase of national and international talent at the newly constructed architectural marvel of a concert house, the Harpa, with a backdrop of snowcapped mountains, and a salty sea breeze is in Reykjavík's Old Harbor. For scheduling information and tickets visit: http://reykjavikjazz.is/

Reykjavik Culture Night
Aug 22nd
Reykjavík Culture Night will be transpiring for the twentieth time on summery August 23rd 2014. Celebrations and festivities are spread wide and far across Reykjavík with music, events and fine art in city streets and squares, museums, businesses, and even in residential gardens! The slogan of the cultural night is "come on in!" So don't get left out if you're in town.

Reykjavik Marathon
Aug 22nd
Íslandsbanki Reykjavík Marathon is an annual race that was established in 1984, and takes place in late August of every year. Registration for this event begins every year in January, with forms being available to participants at http://marathon.is/reykjavik-marathon. This marathon coincides with Reykjavík's Culture Night, with the kick off being proudly held in the city center on the anniversary of Reykjavík City.

SEPTEMBER

Reykjavík International Film Festival
Late September
RIFF is an annual showcase of new and progressive independent films over the span of eleven days in late September. Tickets for a wide range of dramas and non-fiction films from over 40 countries by up-and-coming filmmakers are available at http://en.riff.is/

NOVEMBER

Dagar Myrkurs
Early November
Over a span of ten days in early November, the town of Egilsstaðir celebrates the waning daylight with an event called "Days of Darkness." Locals gather to tell ghost and troll tales during torch illuminated evenings.

JUNE | SUMMER EVENTS

Sjómannadagurinn
First weekend in June
The first weekend of June every ship in Iceland is in the harbor, and every sailor has the day off. Seafarers' Day is a time for music, games, good food, and a great deal of drinking. Be sure to check out the docked ships in the old harbor, and stunning views of Mount Esja across the bay. Don't miss the popular fishermen's tug-of-war competition, rowing races, and other tests of brawn.

Viking Festival in Hafnarfjörður
June 14th-17th
For three days the south west coast of Iceland celebrates the summer solstice, with the oldest and largest festival of its kind. Any and all Viking related aspects of culture are on display for visitors to see. Watch battle re-enactments, marksmanship competitions, and even the occasional Viking wedding. Sing, dance and dine at a multitude of establishments serving up Viking feasts well into the night. Lastly, you may sleep like a Viking at the Hotel Viking, or just head back to Reykjavík; it only 10km away. For info on events visit: http://fjorukrain.is/en/viking-festival

National Independence Day
June 17th is National Day, a day that commemorates Iceland's independence from Denmark and the founding of the Republic of Iceland in June, 1944. It also marks the birthday of Jon Sigurdsson; a steadfast leader with an iconic role in the Icelandic Independence Movement. On this day the streets overflow with an abundance of music, street performances, games and food. Church bells across town are rung in unison at 9:55 am to kick off the day's events, which begin on a solemn note with patriotic displays and speeches, but by mid-afternoon the atmosphere changes to a more celebratory tone. Festivities generally wind down at 7 pm. A parade runs from Austurvöllur to the Suðurgata Cemetery. Entertainment can be had for the entire family at Arnarhóll, and Vikings can be found in Hallargarður.

Suzuki Midnight Sun Run
June 23, 2014
The annual 5k, 10k, and half-marathon Midnight Sun Run, has been going strong for twenty-two years now, and there's no slowing down. Registration begins in January, and all participants are invited to bring their bathing suits and enjoy the Laugardalslaug hot tubs and steam baths free of charge at conclusion of the race.

JULY

Eistnaflug
July 10-12
The Eistnaflug Music Festival is a three-day music festival in Neskaupsstaður, 700km east of the capital city of Reykjavík. It begins on July 9th with a pre-fest, and runs through July 12th. Egilsbúð, the indoor venue is sure to provide a fantastic setting for the event come rain or shine. Be sure to rest up before hand, because when the sun never sets, the party never ends. http://eistnaflug.is/

Jónsmessan, or Midsummer
June 24th
Visitors and locals gather to celebrate the mystical midnight sun on the longest day of the year. The summer solstice ushers in a long month of endless sunshine, and Icelandic folklore will have you believe that good health will come of rolling in dew-covered grass on this night. Organized events are scarce, but many locals celebrate privately and will gladly welcome visitors to partake in bonfires and parties.

The Arctic Open Golf Championship - Akureyri
June 26-28
Since 1986, the Akureyri Golf Club has hosted a tournament known as The Arctic Open Golf Championship. Even if your swing is bad and your score is low, you'll still have something to brag about when you've played golf under the midnight sun at the northernmost golf club in the world. This event attracts golfers from every part of the world, so you'll be sure to make some international friends. Even with an entry fee of $385 USD space is scarce, and reservations need to be made accordingly.
Be sure to visit www.arcticopen.is for more info.

All Tomorrow's Parties
July 10-13
All Tomorrow's Parties is a music festival that goes against the grain of the larger, more commercial music festivals. The event takes place over the span of three days with music playing from 7pm to 2am each day. For more info on pricing, location, and band line-up visit: www.atpfestival.com

Laugavegur Ultra Marathon
July 18
The Laugavegur Ultra Marathon takes runners through a rigorous 55 km multi-terrain course of the majestic natural beauty of Landmannalaugar. Registration opens each year in January, and the Laugavegur Ultra Marathon can be used as a qualifying race for the famous Ultra-trail Du Mont-Blanc. http://marathon.is/ultramarathon

Humarhátíð
End of June
Is an annual port festival held in Hornafirði port of on the last weekend in June. The event celebrates the importance of the Norway Lobster, also know as the Dublin Bay Prawn, to this small fishing community in Höfn. Port Hornafirði is often referred to as the lobster capital of the area, albeit this crustacean is not the typical lobster one most commonly thinks of. This event consists of a family-oriented fair with an abundance of open-air flea markets, dancing and even an ice-sculpting competition.

EVENTS JAN

Rainbow Reykjavík

Jan 30-Feb 2nd

Rainbow Reykjavík is a four day winter pride festival that incorporates all of the wonders Iceland has to offer into an LGBT-friendly tour. Event packages offer a variety of activities, dining options, music, and nightlife events, with a plethora of new international friends to share these once in a lifetime experiences with. More info is available at www.rainbowreykjavik.com/

Þorrablót

Mid January to late February

Þorri is the given name of the fourth winter month in the old Icelandic calander, named thusly after an early Norwegian king. The Kvens, a 12th century minority group in Norway descended from Finnish peasants and fishermen, offered the King Porri a sacrifice each mid-winter, and from this sprang the inspiration for this rather modern festival. This throwback to pagan times has amassed a great deal of publicity over the years, particularly for serving traditional delicacies and oddities that had nearly become extinct in the modern age. If you are lucky enough to be in attendance for this festival, be sure to keep an open mind when sampling the Þorramatur which consists of a wide selection of meat and fish products cured in a traditional manner, served with a side of rúgbrauð (dense rye bread baked in a pot or steamed in special wooden casks by burying them in the ground near a hot spring), butter and brennivín (an Icelandic schnapps).

The Winter Lights Festival

February 6th-15th

If there is light in Reykjavík, and it is not yet summer, you must be a witnessing the splendid illumination of the city during the annual Winter Lights Festival. The entire festival was created to lift the city from its dreary winter blues, with a magnificent display of commissioned light-art. Buildings of prominence shine brightly against a backdrop of gray mountains, dark seas, and a black sky. The festival itself has small, sub-events with themes, some of which include free admission to steam baths and hot springs at Laugardalslaug, Sundhöll, and Grafarvogslaug. In addition to Lágafellslaug and Álftaneslaug swimming pools and Ylströnd thermal beach. Pool Night has indeed become a fan favorite; and with music, entertainment, and pool illuminations, how could it not? Of course, I can't forget about Museum Night, which prominently displays Iceland's heritage and an abundance of local talent in no less than forty museums. To top it all off, I must tell you that it's all free! The admission, the Museum Night bus service that offers unlimited transfers, it's all free and illuminated. To download a PDF schedule of the Museum Night Bus, visit http://winterlightsfestival.is.

FEB

MARCH

Beer Day

March 1st, 1989 marked the end of Prohibition in Iceland. The 1915 ban originally outlawed all forms of alcohol, but was later reduced to apply only to beer with alcohol content greater than 2.25%. By 1985 Icelanders had been getting around the law by adding legal spirits to legal non-alcoholic beers, but soon enough, even this was banned. With support for the Prohibition at an all time low, a new vote was cast drawing an end to the 75 year long ban. If, by chance, you happen to be in Reykjavík on the first of March, or any weekend for that matter, you might encounter the word "rúntur" being thrown around. Rúntur translates into "round turn," and while in the country it's used to describe a bunch of seasonal effective teenagers trying to cure the winter blues by driving circles around town, in the city the term is used to describe a pub crawl. Any one can rúntur, as long as you over twenty; Iceland's legal drinking age. If you are planning to participate in the latter type of rúntur, do like the Icelanders do, and pre-game with the liquor you purchased at the duty-free shop upon landing. There is a reason that all of the locals dash straight away to the grocery carts and begin layering the bottles like Jenga for drunks, the prices are as much as 60% less than what you can expect to pay anywhere on the island.

APRIL

Sumardagurinn Fyrsti

First Thursday after April 18.
At first glance, this public holiday marks the First Day of Summer rather prematurely. However, according to the old Norse calendar, which divided the year into only two seasons, summer is right on time in mid April. Even though temperatures are still quite winter-like in April, Icelanders still rejoice with small locally organized celebrations of music, sporting events, and a brass-led parade.

Reykjavik Arts Festival

May 22nd to June 5th
This annual arts festival is an exhibition of newly commissioned artwork created by hundreds of artists from around the world. For 45 years, the city of Reykjavik has been presenting contemporary and classical works in innovative, interactive, and, often times, surprising places for two weeks out of the year. Because of its wide variety of nationally and internationally created art, the Reykjavík Arts Festival has been the catalyst for cultural diversity and development in Iceland. For information and scheduling about concerts, theater performances, exhibitions, and operas
visit: http://en.listahatid.is/

MAY

GENERAL INDEX

Akureyri, 49, 51, 54, 92
Askja, 54, 90
Airport, 29

Banks, 13
Basic Guide, 13
Blue Lagoon, 43, 54, 58

Calendar of Events, 104-109
Car Rental, 18, 23
Currency, 12

Driving, 19, 20, 21,
Dettifoss, 46, 54, 83

Egilsstaðir, 45
Electrical, 16
Embassy, 16, 17
Eyjafjallajökull, 42, 54, 76

F-Roads, 22, 52-53
Fuel, 21
Food, 27, 97

Gas Cards, 14
Geysir, 35, 54
Glacier Climbing, 95
Groceries, 14
Gullfoss, 34, 54, 70

Hallgrímskirkja, 54, 57
Hallormsstaður Forest, 45, 54, 82
Hekla, 36, 38, 54, 72
Höfn, 44
Hveragerði Geothermal Park, 60
Hveraröndor Hverir, 84

Icelandic Delicacies, 96
Insurance, 19
Itineraries, 22-51

Jökulsárlón, 40, 54

Krafla, 46, 54, 88
Krýsuvík Geothermal Area, 32, 60

Language, 12
Landmannalaugar, 39, 54, 73
Lakagígar, 54, 81
Laundry, 15

Money, 12
Mývatn Lake, 46, 49, 54, 87

Öxarárfoss, 65
Öxarár River, 65

Restaurants, 98-103
Reykjadalur (Smoke Valley), 36, 61
Reykjavík, 30-31, 33-34

Selatangar Ruins, 33, 61
Seljalandsfoss, 37, 54, 74
Seyðisfjörður, 45, 46, 54, 82
Skaftafell Visitors Center, 40
Skógafoss, 37, 54, 74
Strokkur, 68

Þingvellir (Thingvellir) National Park, 62-67
Þingvallavatn Lake (Thingvallavatn), 65-66
Þingvalla (Thingvalla) Kirkja, 66

Vatnajökull National Park, 40, 54, 78
Vík í Mýrdal, 40, 54, 80

CPSIA information can be obtained at www.ICGtesting.com
Printed in the USA
LVOW05s0215150515

438417LV00017B/99/P